Understanding Librarians

CHANDOS
INFORMATION PROFESSIONAL SERIES

Series Editor: Ruth Rikowski
(email: Rikowskigr@aol.com)

Chandos' new series of books is aimed at the busy information professional. They have been specially commissioned to provide the reader with an authoritative view of current thinking. They are designed to provide easy-to-read and (most importantly) practical coverage of topics that are of interest to librarians and other information professionals. If you would like a full listing of current and forthcoming titles, please visit our website www.chandospublishing.com or email info@chandospublishing.com or telephone +44 (0) 1223 499140.

New authors: we are always pleased to receive ideas for new titles; if you would like to write a book for Chandos, please contact Dr Glyn Jones on email gjones@chandospublishing.com or telephone number +44 (0) 1993 848726.

Bulk orders: some organisations buy a number of copies of our books. If you are interested in doing this, we would be pleased to discuss a discount. Please contact on e-mail info@chandospublishing.com or telephone +44 (0) 1223 499140.

Understanding Librarians

Communication is the issue

BARBARA HULL
WITH CONTRIBUTIONS FROM MARION
CHURKOVICH, CHRISTINE OUGHTRED
AND DENISE TURNER

Oxford Cambridge New Delhi

Chandos Publishing
Hexagon House
Avenue 4
Station Lane
Witney
Oxford OX28 4BN
UK
Tel: +44 (0) 1993 848726
Email: info@chandospublishing.com
www.chandospublishing.com

Chandos Publishing is an imprint of Woodhead Publishing Limited

Woodhead Publishing Limited
80 High Street
Sawston
Cambridge CB22 3HJ
UK
Tel: +44 (0) 1223 499140
Fax: +44 (0) 1223 832819
www.woodheadpublishing.com

First published in 2011

ISBN:
978 1 84334 615 9

British Library Cataloguing-in-Publication Data.
A catalogue record for this book is available from the British Library.

The publishers make no representation, express or implied, with regard to the accuracy of the information contained in this publication and cannot accept any legal responsibility or liability for any errors or omissions.

The material contained in this publication constitutes general guidelines only and does not represent to be advice on any particular matter. No reader or purchaser should act on the basis of material contained in this publication without first taking professional advice appropriate to their particular circumstances. All screenshots in this publication are the copyright of the website owner(s), unless indicated otherwise.

Typeset by RefineCatch Limited, Bungay, Suffolk
Printed in the UK and USA.

Printed in the UK by 4edge Limited - www.4edge.co.uk

This book is dedicated to Bill, my lifelong partner,
who probably values libraries even more than I do myself.

Contents

List of tables

About the author and contributors

Barbara Hull

Dr. Barbara Hull is the author of the British Library-commissioned Report 'Barriers to Libraries as agents of lifelong learning' For many years she has demonstrated a simultaneous enthusiasm for both library management and teaching – a range of subjects including information literacy skills, inviting the epithet 'poacher *and* gamekeeper'.

Her first experience of working in libraries was as an assistant in a UK university library in the 1960s. She then became an undergraduate herself and gained an Honours degree in French Studies from Manchester University in 1972. After qualifying as a teacher in 1973, she began her teaching career, teaching French and Latin in secondary schools and French in Adult and Community Education.

In 1977, while still maintaining her involvement in adult education, she qualified as a librarian at the then Manchester Polytechnic and she went on to gain valuable experience as a librarian in a special library where she devised a unique retrieval system. She then became the librarian in a tertiary college, where she was responsible for setting up the library from the college's inception. Here, after observing students' very minimal information handling skills, she started to teach a library studies course.

In 1986 she was awarded an MA from Salford University, her thesis being a study of the impact of architectural design on the functioning of two large public libraries.

Her awareness of the problems faced by the adult learner has grown throughout her working life. The life-changing effects of involvement in adult education, observed in the field, led to formal research at the University of Leeds, where in 1997 she was awarded a PhD for her thesis, 'Changes in the self concepts of adult students with special reference to previous educational disadvantage'.

In tandem with her role as Senior Tutor Librarian at a large further education college, she also taught French, English and job seeking skills. She was appointed as Social Sciences Librarian at Teesside University in 1992, a position which involved a heavy teaching load of Information Handling skills. Becoming increasingly sensitised to the very crucial role played by libraries in the education process and the communication barriers which can impede access to information she applied to the British Library for research funding in this area and in 1998, as the result of a competitive bid, she was awarded funding to conduct a large scale research project. This resulted in the publication of the British Library report, 'Barriers to Libraries as agents of lifelong learning' and generated numerous journal publications and international conference presentations, a number by invitation.

In 2000, updating her interest in language teaching, she qualified as an ESOL teacher and subsequently taught the 'English for Learning' module to non-native speakers of English at Teesside University, where in 2003 she was nominated as the university's first Associate Teaching Fellow. She was awarded a Trinity College Diploma in ESOL in 2005 and is currently a Trinity international ESOL examiner, working mainly in Europe.

Dr. Hull may be contacted at the Social Futures Institute, Teesside University, Middlesbrough TS1 3BA, UK (b.hull@ tees.ac.uk).

Christine Oughtred and **Marion Churkovich** are Liaison librarians for Faculty of Arts and Education, Deakin University, Geelong campus at Waurn Ponds.
Contact details: *marion.churkovich@deakin.edu.au*
christine.oughtred@deakin.edu.au

Denise Turner is currently Assistant Director (Learning and Research Support) at Teesside University. Before moving to Teesside she worked in public libraries and further education. Since joining the University she has developed her interest in education and qualified as a teacher. She has co-authored papers on information literacy and methods of assessment. She was recently a member of a JISC funded project on study skills (UKAN-SKILLS). Her interests include e-learning, the use of educational technology and information literacy. Contact details: *d.turner@tees.ac.uk*.

Defining the problem

Abstract: This chapter explains the ideas behind the impetus to write this book. It considers the concern regarding communication failure in general, the traditional mismatch between expert and layman and some observations on ameliorating the problems. It contains a brief synopsis of the book as a whole.

Key words: communication failure, libraries, expert and layman.

Rationale for this book

Many useful and erudite books have been written by librarians, to advise and guide librarians. Many have been written by librarians as guides to non-librarians in their quests for information. Understandably, however clearly expressed, these books are written primarily from a librarian's perspective. Our view of the world is formed by our experience. As a practising librarian of many years standing, with qualifications and extensive experience in other areas of endeavour (schoolteacher, adult educator, tax officer, to name some) I believe that I may be in the privileged position of having access to a variety of perspectives which have informed the writing of this book, which is written with the intention of improving understanding and communication between librarians and others.

Broad overview of failure in communication

Over the last half century there has been much discussion on the concept of communication, or rather of *non*-communication: in 1950s and 1960s Europe, the 'Theatre of the Absurd' promoted to the intelligentsia the idea that, as human existence has no purpose, all communication has no meaning, breaks down, and results finally in silence. From a less extreme perspective, social commentators have more recently lamented the lack of 'connectedness' in developed societies, particularly the USA: people are communicating less via groups and societies, resulting in a reduction in trust, and a loss of what is termed social-capital. According to Putnam (1995), 'There is reason to believe that deep-seated techno-logical trends are radically "privatizing" or "individualizing" our use of leisure time and thus disrupting many opportunities for social-capital formation.' It is a paradox that we have a media-saturated society where people no longer speak to each other. The problem is clearly of concern to some. At the last New Year, instead of the usual health wealth and happiness, I was wished 'A year of communication'!

However, the human failure to communicate has a much longer pedigree than the 21st century. Witnessing people talking at cross purposes has long been a traditional source of comedy: I have only to think of my mother and mother-in-law, enjoying a 'conversation' at total cross purposes at a family get together, to raise a smile; theatre plays as far back as Shakespeare's and beyond are full of examples of communication failure. It has evidently long been present in society so we may conclude that it is endemic. This book aims to highlight some of the factors contributing to the communication problems in the library setting and suggest ways of alleviating them.

In everyday interactions, most of us would recognise that there often exists a gulf between expert and layman which can make communication problematical. How many of us have been 'blinded with science' by the diagnosis of an expert doctor who describes our condition in arcane medical jargon? Or the utterances of a car mechanic whose description of why our car engine is no longer working leaves us none the wiser? Usually the 'expert' is quite unaware of the consternation he is causing, although it is not unknown for someone 'in the know' to enjoy the discomfort of the non-expert: an often portrayed example of this behaviour is the waiter in a pricey restaurant with the menu written in French, who sometimes sneers at a customer for being unable to decipher the menu or corrects their poor pronunciation (a well-loved source of comedy for script writers).

Professionals frequently make unwitting assumptions about other people's pre-existing knowledge in their own particular subject area, and this includes information professionals. However, in common with other caring professions, those organising and ostensibly facilitating access to information must never lose sight of the fact that the rest of the world is not composed of information experts with the same values as ourselves. Walter and Mediavilla (2005) remind us of 'the seemingly galactic gaps in communication that can occur when people with different values and worldviews try to have a dialogue'.

Each and every individual has a unique Weltanschauung,[1] resulting from his life experiences, that acts as a filter through which he views the world, and is frequently unaware that others may not share this same view. It can cause problems when expert professionals fail to recognise the phenomenon when interacting with non-experts. Thankfully in recent years there has been recognition of the problem in some areas, and, in UK medical consultations for example, there is usually a genuine attempt to offer explanations in layman's terms. As information professionals, often working with the latest information and communication technologies, we need to remember that what is commonplace and normal for us can be totally alien and cause consternation to non-professionals.

Many other factors conspire to block communication. Differences in national culture can be a source of barriers – this is becoming more relevant for everyone, including information providers, as more people move around the globe for the purposes of study or employment. According to Prof. Geert Hofstede, Emeritus Professor, Maastricht University, 'Culture is more often a source of conflict than of synergy. Cultural differences are a nuisance at best and often a disaster' (ITIM International website, 2010).

The term 'nonstandard user' has sometimes been used by librarians to indicate those users who may require extra help. What is a 'nonstandard user'? We might well try to define a standard user! A truly standard user does not exist, any more than the average man does; it would feel extremely unnerving to meet someone completely average in every respect, without any peculiarities or idiosyncrasies. However, on a less philosophical note, it is recognised that there are some areas where differences, personal and perceptual, can generate communication problems which we may be able to predict and therefore partially circumvent.

Overview of subsequent chapters

This volume seeks to remind colleagues of a number of factors which may conspire to interfere with librarian–client interactions. First, there is still a major misunderstanding of the purpose of libraries; Chapter 2 'What are libraries for?'

explores the perception of libraries from the perspective of providers and clients and how they can mismatch. As a profession we have long had an image problem, from both our own viewpoint and that of others: it is quite common, when asked what they 'do' at parties, for young librarians to conceal their true job, afraid that they will be seen as boring. Similarly, when, as an experienced lecturer, I told my Adult Education classes that I was leaving to train as a librarian the comment came, 'What a waste!' Chapter 3, 'Images of librarians', explores these issues.

Using, or not using, a library is part of life and when they enter our portals, people bring with them their whole self, including all the psychological baggage they normally carry around. Chapter 4, 'Psychological barriers', looks at some of the reasons for the way people act in the library setting.

In many societies how a person thinks and acts is often dictated by their social class; in the UK, for example, where the class system is still quite prevalent, the labouring classes have always tended to be less interested in libraries than the middle classes. Originally, part of the reason for this was an innate suspicion for anything provided by their 'oppressors', i.e. the establishment and more recently perhaps the perception that libraries are for the middle classes, evidenced by the fact that most librarians are middle class. Inextricably linked to social class is educational achievement, with a measurable difference in the educational achievement between the social classes, due in part to expectations, both personal and societal. These ideas are expanded in Chapter 5, 'Social class and lack of education as barriers'.

A growing source of possible interference with library – client communication is the English language itself! Not of course the structure and content of English per se, which has been lauded for the wealth of its word count, which facilitates the precise identification of objects and concepts, especially in scientific areas: according to its publishers, the Second Edition of the 20-volume Oxford English Dictionary contains full entries for 171,476 words in current use, and 47,156 obsolete words (Oxford dictionaries, 2011). This may be compared with 100,000 entries for the French language reference Grand Robert (Robert, 2011).

A further point is that there are many 'Englishes', so that even native speakers from different parts of the world may experience misunderstanding. As George Bernard Shaw, the Irish playwright, observed long ago, England and America are two countries separated by a language. When the internationally famous brass band from the north of England, the Black Dyke Band,[2] did a tour of the US, some people were surprised that the musicians did not look quite as they had expected!

English has been dubbed the world's lingua franca, but, given the volume of lexis, not to mention the idiosyncrasies of syntax and grammar, it should be recognised that to learn English is no mean feat. But, there are other underlying tensions for a non-native speaker speaking in English to a native speaker, a subconscious given that the language is being spoken because it is superior and by extension that the native speaker is in some way superior. Although most liberally-minded individuals would strongly refute this, these ideas still appear to be present in the collective psyche – probably a throwback to the days of the Empire. When one considers the intellectual effort and sheer determination needed to learn another language to the point where one can function fully and normally in a society – a qualification not many English native speakers achieve, the real candidate for superiority is the one who has learned or is learning a second language. Therefore there is a chapter (Chapter 6) entitled 'Language as a barrier'.

If a person cannot swim, they are not likely to go to a swimming pool, or if they are persuaded to do so they are likely to experience apprehension in that place. Similarly those who have weak, or non-existent, literacy and numeracy skills will have to summon an enormous amount of courage to enter the place where their inadequacies will be most visible, a place which is the shrine to the printed word and often arranged in numerical order. More currently, with public libraries often being the designated site for information and communication technology, those who have been left behind by technological developments, possibly through unemployment and/or poverty, will also need to be brave to expose their lack of expertise. These issues are dealt with in two chapters, 'Lack of literacy and numeracy skills as a barrier' (Chapter 7) and 'Information and communication technology as a barrier' (Chapter 8).

Over the past half century the world has changed considerably and, thankfully in some ways, for the better. The changes in attitudes towards disability, in terms of reference, have been seismic. As a child in the UK I often heard the term 'cripple' used, with no offence intended, whereas today most people in the UK and the USA would eschew such language. Similarly, the acronym ESN was used to denote 'Educationally sub normal', but with the advent of greater awareness this was cleverly recycled into 'Educational special needs' which has now changed to 'learning difficulties' in the USA or 'specific learning difficulties' in the UK. Such lexical changes may be interpreted as an indication of greater sensitivity to the problems faced by those with disabilities. Even better, there has been legislation in many parts of the world for practical steps to be taken to improve the quality of life for the disabled. But all of this is relatively new and some of the older ideas and prejudices, not to mention unsuitable premises, still persist to create barriers, and this is considered more fully in Chapter 9, 'Disability as a barrier'.

The possible remedies for all these barriers are discussed in the second part of the book. Any psychologist or 'life coach' will tell us that, for any human endeavour to succeed there must to be a clear idea of desired goals. A lot of human effort can be dissipated through a lack of clear direction and, in the case of team endeavours, leadership: these ideas are explored further in Chapter 10, 'Clarity of purpose'.

Towards the end of the last century there was a surge in the culture of evaluation, leading sometimes to a knee-jerk administration of user satisfaction forms, but meaningful evaluation must be a more thoughtful activity if it is to underpin any improvement to service. Chapter 11, 'Evaluation and the value of systematic research', takes these ideas further.

Our species is named 'Homo sapiens', thinking man (with apologies to all thinking women). One of the essential attributes and joys of being human is the ability to reflect, to reflect on something we have witnessed or done, and conceive of how it might have been done differently. In the last half century this act of reflection has been brought to the fore in the lives of professionals: we are no longer expected to accept unreservedly the wisdom inherited from the past, but to consider how we are performing, reflect on this and make any changes we believe will improve our performance. This is the subject of Chapter 12, 'Librarians as reflective practitioners'.

As it is assumed that most people reading this book will be responsible for organising and overseeing the work of others, consideration is given to this in Chapter 13, 'Staff development'.

We live in straitened times. At the time of writing, in the UK and other developed countries, there is pressure to cut expenditure on public services, and the misinformed usually see libraries as a soft target. Now, more than ever, we need to ensure that communities appreciate our worth and are prepared to support us, which is more likely to happen if we already have strong links with them. These ideas are expanded in Chapter 14, 'Self publicise'.

Librarians have a variety of roles to play in the communities they serve; on the one hand they have to be up to speed on the latest in information provision and the means of accessing it; conversely they need highly developed 'people skills' as they may well be in contact with the most 'informationally naïve' of their community.

Included in this volume are contributions from current practitioners which, I believe, represent good practices in satisfaction of these two roles. Chapter 15, 'Breaking down the library walls: responding to the needs of the Google generation', by my colleague Denise Turner at Teesside University UK, recognises the need for making contact with users and describes two case studies, an outreach project, Librarians2U; and the second, which takes advantage of meeting the 'Google generation' on their own ground, describes and evaluates the design and implementation of a learning object developed to be used as a tool to test critical thinking skills.

Chapter 16, the second guest chapter, 'Communication within partnerships at Deakin University Library: the liaison link', is by two Australian colleagues, Christine Oughtred and Marion Churkovich at Deakin University. It focuses on the vital importance of good communication and describes how positive communication can inform partnerships and improve outcomes. It describes three projects: Librarian in residence, Research training and a community-based project at the Institute of Koorie Education, designed to enable Aboriginal and Torres Strait Islander students to study without being removed from their communities for substantial periods of time.

The subject matter of Chapter 17, 'Where are we now?' is, I think, self evident.

Notes

1. View of the world.
2. *http://www.blackdykeband.co.uk/3/* (accessed 19/01/11).

References

ITIM International website, *www.geert-hofstede.com* (accessed 29/08/10).

Oxford Dictionaries (2011) *www.oxforddictionaries.com/page/93* (accessed 19/01/11).

Putnam, R.D. (1995) 'Bowling Alone: America's Declining Social Capital', *Journal of Democracy*, January 1995, pp. 65–78.

Robert (2011) *www.lerobert.com/espace-numerique/enligne/le-grand-robert-de-la-langue-francaise-en-ligne-12-mois.html* (accessed 19/01/11).

Walter, V.A. and Mediavilla, C. (2005) 'Teens are from Neptune, librarians are from Pluto: an analysis of online reference transactions', *Library Trends*, 54, 2, pp. 209–27.

2

What are libraries for?

Abstract: This chapter examines varying conceptions of the purpose of libraries, focusing particularly on the public library as a key player, and explores how differing conceptions can affect communication between information providers and their clients.

Key words: purpose of libraries, public libraries, changes in library use.

Perceived purpose of libraries

What are libraries for? What do librarians/information professionals do? Although these are by no means new questions, they are pertinent to readers of this work. As librarians we need to remind ourselves that the information provider's conception of the library and that of its users do not necessarily concur. A serious mismatch can exist between client and professional, between the client's expectations and awareness of a library's potential and the reality of both in technical and financial terms. Some clients have an unrealistically inflated idea of what can be made available to them but, tragically, many others remain unaware of the true potential of libraries. Communicating the purpose of one's own particular library is part of the role of an information professional, a part that is easily neglected in favour of more pressing routine matters.

Public libraries

Much of the debate concerns the role of the public library but this is relevant, not only to public librarians, but to all information providers: for many of our clients the public library is their first contact with the world of information provision and information professionals. This situation is a double-edged sword: if that initial contact was a positive one, their mental image of libraries will reflect this and will provide a good basis for further contact. However, if their previous library experience only involved visiting a small branch library, however positive that experience may have been, they may have acquired a somewhat truncated impression of the global potential of libraries. Someone accustomed to using a small library stock, where the retrieval system can be bypassed and items located through browsing, may experience problems when faced with a large university library. Hull (2000) found, for example, that for female students there was a statistically significant relationship between their having difficulties in physically locating items on the shelves in the university library and being a member of the public library.

Development of public libraries in the UK

Clearly the public library, with either positive or negative connotations, forms a part of the Weltanschauung[1] of many, if not all, citizens of the developed world. But old memories die hard; when the Hollywood actor Kirk Douglas, a son of Russian Jewish immigrants, told his father about the free public library in the early part of the 20th century, his father refused to believe the existence of such a place: a place where you could freely browse a collection of books and then take them home, *for free!* A strange echo of this incredulity occurred recently, nearly a century later, in a public library in Darlington, northern England, when a young boy brought in his father, who asked the librarian 'Is it really all free?'

When the public library service was first conceived in the UK, it was driven by a paternalistic motive to provide a sober, improving pastime to the new urban working classes – mainly to save them from the 'demon drink'. The plan was not entirely successful in that the British working classes are still not generally known for their love of temperance. In addition, rather than serving the working classes, many public library services were soon colonised by the more articulate and demanding middle classes, to create a service perceived by many of the working classes as irrelevant to them. Over the years this situation has generated a backlash and a demand that public libraries should serve the needs of the entire community which they purport to serve. This debate is ongoing.

In 1998, the then UK Culture Secretary, Chris Smith, was still promoting the 'official' definition of libraries as 'the people's universities ... entirely egalitarian places. The Duke and the dustman can walk through the door and be treated the same way' (Watson, 1998). There are many who would disagree with this rosy view, and who maintain that the public library's efforts to be welcoming to all have been, at best, lukewarm, failing to be inclusive of the working classes and other socially excluded groups. In consequence, the public library service in the UK has continued to be used more by the, generally more assertive, middle classes and to reflect their values and answer their needs. Some would go as far as to portray the public library as a servant of the class system and argue, 'that the class system pervades every aspect of society, including library usage ... that libraries themselves are a means of social control and are therefore alien to working class life and rejected by working class people' (Muddiman and others, 2000).

Many library users are still rooted in the idea of publicly funded libraries as a force for self-improvement and not for entertainment:

> It amazes me that we have to go on insisting on this. The idea of a free library presupposes the value, to the individual and to society, of reading, and the value of reading presupposes the value of books. If we fill a library with potboilers and that genre of contemporary literature described as crossover because it crosses us over from maturity to infancy, we abandon the grand educative function which libraries were philanthropically invented to serve. First, the serious books give way to footling books, then the books give way altogether to something else. Records, tapes, CDs, DVDs, and now computers. (Jacobson, 2005)

The worst fears of Jacobson and others, who believe that the true function of public libraries is no longer being served by the purchase of non-book materials, are confirmed on perusal of the LISU statistics (2005) for England which record a huge increase in the issue of video stock for the five years to 2004: 32 per cent for English counties, 35 per cent for unitary authorities, 33 per cent for metropolitan districts and 24 per cent for London (Table 2.17a). This is matched in the same areas by a huge fall in the number of books issued for the same period: down by 25 per cent, 27 per cent, 25 per cent and 24 per cent respectively (Table 2.15a).

However, without a doubt UK public libraries, in the wake of the economic downturn, are changing: some are closing down, others are being transformed into something which no longer fulfils many people's mental picture of what a library should be. In a March 2010 interview with Margaret Hodge, the then Minister of State for Culture and Tourism, Stuart Jeffries, reported:

> She told me that running a successful public library in the 21st century is tough. Technological advances and higher expectations of service mean that libraries must, in her glum progressivist phrase, 'move with the times to stay part of the times'. 'I do care passionately about libraries,' she says, 'but they have to change. The footfall is down and book issues are massively down. Only 14 of 151 local authorities have libraries that offer ebooks.' (Jeffries, 2010)

Changed perceptions of libraries

Should the role of libraries be changing? The format of materials has clearly moved on from the etymological origin of the word, librum, a book. Most librarians would agree that it is the content, not the format, which is important. Was it too great an insistence on the book form that led to the perceived rejection of libraries by the younger generation? Was it an attempt to reflect diversification of format which led so many university libraries to change their names to learning resource centres? It is interesting that a number have now reverted to being libraries, possibly because no-one understood what a learning resource centre was. In the UK, public libraries are currently revamping themselves with new names – 'Explore', 'Inspire'; even 'palazzo of human thought' (Jeffries 2010) has been mooted! Will anyone realise what these places are?

Total rejection of the book form calls up a very pertinent quote, variously attributed, which is worth repeating: there are two kinds of fools: one says, 'This is old, therefore it is good,' and the other says, 'This is new, therefore it is better.' It behoves information providers to keep a sense of proportion in deciding format and not be bedazzled by the latest technological advance: in some situations the printed book can still be a clear winner.

It is argued by some that after tempting the non-user through the door with the prospect of the latest technology, librarians can then coax them into 'self improvement'. A sign in a northeast England library temptingly offers 'Borrow 3 books and you can borrow a DVD free' (borrowing the DVD normally costs £2 per week) – is this the equivalent of 'Eat your greens and you can have chocolate'? Or perhaps it is a somewhat cynical acceptance of the inevitable preference for non-book materials and an attempt to manipulate the otherwise ailing book issue statistics.

Libraries as instruments of social engineering

It is perhaps worthwhile reiterating that the demand for public libraries did not come from the working classes – at whom they were originally targeted – but from the middle classes who were concerned with the way the working classes were spending their free time: the Capitalist economic model had created shift patterns that left workers with free time, which had not been the case with the agrarian model. The thrust to create public libraries was prompted more by Victorian middle class paternalism than by demand from the lower social orders (McMenemy, 2009). Campaigners felt that encouraging the lower classes to spend their free time on morally uplifting activities, such as reading, rather than drinking in public houses, would promote greater social good. This original intended purpose of public library provision has persisted in the collective psyche: there is a quite widespread belief among public librarians and users that part of the role of the public library is to educate. For a certain sector, albeit a minority, of the working classes the public library has provided a lifeline to self improvement, a route for the self-motivated to escape from the class in which they were born. Muddiman (1999) elaborates this aspect: 'What do working class and disadvantaged people think of libraries, and how are they valuable to them?' In 1993, Usherwood compiled a booklet celebrating national library week entitled, 'Success Stories: Libraries are Full of Them', in which a mix of Yorkshire celebrities and the not so famous, many with working-class roots, commented at length on what libraries had meant to them in terms of education, life changes and so on. These extracts make fascinating reading, in the main because their dominant discourse is transparently one of individual improvement and enlightenment and what Alan Bennett sums up as 'the theme of escape' (Usherwood, 1993, p. 6). Richard Hoggart's contribution to the booklet is one of the most explicit: comparing Hunslet Public Library to his grammar school, he describes it as a 'wonderful air-hole'. For Hoggart, the key purpose of the library for a bright working class boy like himself was individual enlightenment, escape to a wider world, and social mobility. Such values, of course, were fundamental to mid-century British social democracy and still, for many, constitute the fundamental rationale of the public library service.

The idea of libraries as instruments of social engineering is a persistent one: according to Black (2000), 'the 150th anniversary of the passing of the first Public Libraries Act in Britain offers an opportunity to examine one aspect of public library history which has tended to be swept under the carpet; namely the question as to whether public libraries could ever be described as truly classless rather than the preserve of a particular social class. Although the welfare state has encouraged many people, not least librarians, to view public libraries as a service offered freely to all, regardless of class, it could be argued that they have always been, and continue to be, an expression of liberal middle-class ideals'.

In Germany the public library also has a traditionally educative role: 'Public libraries in Germany are seeking to enumerate advancement of information literacy as one of their core activities. They traditionally invest in the promotion of literacy and reading which can be appreciated as *conditio sine qua non* to information literacy' (vom Orde and Wein, 2009).

A degree of ambiguity of purpose also exists in some college libraries that offer a certain amount of recreational materials, in addition to materials in support of course work, hoping to draw in the less academic students. As the academic ones would go anyway, this provision of leisure materials can lead to confusion in their minds as to the true function of the library: if the college library is providing leisure materials, why does it not stock the latest blockbuster?

Besides being custodians and facilitators to accessing human knowledge, libraries frequently serve as a focal centre for a community and thus have a secondary role as a social centre; it is an essentially respectable environment which any member of the community can be seen entering. Just how much importance this secondary role should be allowed to assume is open to debate. Should precious floor space be taken from the library to provide a coffee bar, especially in a vicinity such as a city centre where there is already a plentiful number of coffee bars?

In this chapter, where we have considered what libraries are for, perhaps the last word should go to the man in the street or, rather, on the Internet: 'With the exception of university and school libraries, I think city/town libraries serve no purpose in today's society and are a tax drain as:

- Most people have access to the Internet in their own homes or in Internet cafes to find information.
- Most people access books for free through Google or purchase them from Amazon or eBay.

In my town, there are 3 libraries within 3 miles of one another and each is empty of people. Why are they open and why are they using money which should be going to under-funded schools?' ('Are Libraries outdated and do they waste tax money?', Yahoo, 2010).

The current changes in technology and the restrictions on public funding are leading to huge changes in information provision: choice of stock and services seen as appropriate to the majority of the client group. As mentioned earlier, for example, there are more visual materials and less printed. There is always a time lapse before these changes filter through to some laypeople, especially the more senior clients, who are still likely to retain their original concept of the library.

So, when a client walks through the door, is there a match between the mindset of the librarian at the desk and that of the client: what the library is for, how far and in what ways can it help him satisfy his information needs? The librarian needs to be sensitive to the possibility of a *mis*match.

Note

1. View of the world.

References

Black, A. (2000) 'Skeleton in the cupboard: social class and the public library in Britain through 150 years', *Library History* 16 (1) May 2000, pp. 3–12.

Hull, B. (2000) 'Barriers to Libraries as agents of lifelong learning', Library and Information Commission, available at *http://lis.tees.ac.uk/research/researchbh.cfm* (accessed 23/09/10).

Jacobson, H. (2005) 'What are libraries for? Tramps, filth and erudition – not soul-destroying detritus', *Independent*, 22 October 2005, available at *www.independent.co.uk/opinion/commentators/howard-jacobson/howard-jacobson-what-are-libraries-for-tramps-filth-and-erudition—not-souldestroying-detritus-511988.html* (accessed 11/8/10).

Jeffries, S. (2010) 'The battle of Britain's libraries. Coffee shops, gigs, free cinema tickets, flashy architecture . . . is this the future of our libraries? Stuart Jeffries on government plans to shake things up ? and the people standing in their way', *Guardian*, 8 March 2010, available at *www.guardian.co.uk/books/2010/mar/07/future-british-libraries-margaret-hodge* (accessed 11/8/10).

LISU (2005) *LISU Annual Library Statistics 2005 featuring Trend Analysis of UK Public & Academic Libraries 1994–2004*, Public Library Statistics.

McMenemy, D. (2009) *The Public Library*, London: FACET.

Muddiman, D. (1999) 'Images of exclusion: User and community perceptions of the public library', Public Library Policy and Social Exclusion Working Papers, Working Paper Number 9. Leeds, UK: School of Information Management, Leeds Metropolitan University.

Muddiman, D. (2000) 'Open to All? The Public Library and Social Exclusion', Library and Information Commission Research Report 84. Resource: The Council for Museums, Archives and Libraries.

Usherwood, B. (ed.) (1993), *Success stories: libraries are full of them*, Sheffield: Yorkshire and Humberside Branch of the Library Association.

vom Orde, H. and Wein, M. F. (2009) *Information Literacy: an international state of the art*. Germany: IFLA, available at *www.ifla.org/en/publications/information-literacy-state-of-the-art-germany* (accessed 26/08/10).

Watson, D. (1998) 'Man of the people's universities', *Library Association Record*, 100(3) March 98, p. 142.

Yahoo (2010) *http://uk.answers.yahoo.com/question/index?qid=20100508161432AAQlcl3* (accessed 26/08/10).

3

Images of librarians

Abstract: This chapter examines the images of librarians, derived from self perception and the perception of others. It considers how these images may interfere with the optimisation of librarians' professional skills.

Key words: librarian images, stereotypes of librarians.

Reputation is rarely proportioned to virtue[1]

Many librarians have a serious image problem, both from a personal point of view and the perceived view of others. The stereotype most commonly portrayed in the media, besides being extremely irritating and even quite hurtful because of its inaccuracy, can constitute a major barrier to job fulfilment and satisfaction. Most people would not approach a bun-wearing 'shusher' or wimpish mama's boy for help, if they could possibly manage without it.

Problems with media portrayal

Librarians feel targeted by the media when shorthand for a stuffy image is needed: 'like a librarian at a breakdancers convention' ('Image', 1985). 'As early as 1909, a librarian used the word "stereotype" in objecting to the portrayal of her profession in fiction. She complained that librarians were depicted in extremes, either as "old fogy bookworms" or as "unreasonably attractive young people"' (McReynolds, 1985). Apart from crushed egos, does a negative image matter? In sheer financial terms, yes, possibly: it has been cited as adversely affecting the profession, leading to downgrading of jobs ('Image', 1986). This may be due to the fact that often the most visible staff in a library are the clerical staff; this leads subconsciously to the formation of the image of a merely clerical occupation, either stamping out books, in days of yore, or issuing with a scanner, like a supermarket checkout operator. We are all familiar with the incredulous enquiry, 'Do you really need a degree to do that job?' There is also the perception of librarians as perfectionists; control freaks who want to classify and pigeonhole the whole of human experience, a view not entirely without foundation given the desire to be able to easily retrieve a specific piece of information. This can be intimidating for the less well organised; I did once meet a charming student librarian who organised her wardrobe alphabetically: blouses/cardigans/ dresses, etc. That must have been rather intimidating for her flatmates. Highly developed organisational abilities are a prerequisite to being a successful librarian, but we should also remember also that *ars est celare artem*.[2] In a well run information service the client does not need to be party to the details involved but aware of the power of what is possible; in the best works of art the audience is not distracted by the artist's technique, but responds instead to the power of the work.

According to Seale (2008), public perceptions of librarians are somewhat different from media stereotypes:

> Although librarians are often described in positive terms, there is nearly no awareness as to the knowledge, duties, skills, and education of librarians. Although the

connection between media representations and public perceptions has not been systematically researched, the evidence suggests that due to the lack of substantive representations of librarians that highlight their professionalism, public perceptions draw more heavily on stereotypical representations of librarians' personalities. The observed effects on how individuals approach and use librarians and libraries echo this lack of substantive representations and abundance of stereotypical depictions. Ultimately, librarians and libraries tend to not be effectively utilized, as users remain unaware of librarians' abilities and responsibilities.

Positive appraisal of librarians

We should remember that the value of libraries has always been recognised, e.g.: 'Even the most misfitting child, who's chanced upon the library's worth, sits with the genius of the earth, and turns the key to the whole world' (Hughes, 1997). And the keepers of the keys are of course librarians! Librarians have been perceived in a variety of guises, not just negative ones; some more recent ones trail an awesome degree of responsibility in their wake: overwhelmingly, we are seen as information providers, capable of opening up the channels of access to satisfy our clients' needs. The extent of our powers can be perceived as boundless: 'With time and a kindly librarian, any unskilled person can learn how to build a replica of the Taj Mahal' (Angelou, 2002). According to the then Library and Information Commission, libraries and library staff, 'make inclusion happen everywhere for everyone' (Library and Information Commission, 2000) and 'For the first time, in modern history at least, the skills of the information worker have become recognised as pivotal to the conduct of research' (Booth and Brice, 2004).

Librarians should not feel too concerned or hurt by negative media stereotypes of the profession, although hackles do tend to rise when the results for a Google search for 'Librarian images' appears on screen! Similar jokey depictions are made about other professions: at least librarians are not usually subjected to the soft porn treatment often afforded to doctors and nurses!

Librarians as teachers

It is now widely agreed that it is no longer sufficient for librarians to be custodians and organisers of information: in an environment of widening participation in education, social inclusion initiatives and more complex ways of accessing information, teaching skills are seen as desirable. As librarians add another string to their bow by taking on a teaching role, the responsibility becomes even greater! The potential influence of teachers, for good or ill, is legendary: 'A teacher effects eternity; he can never know where his influence stops' (Adams, 1918). Outstanding teachers are sometimes remembered decades later: a 66-year-old male student on a pre-retirement course reported, 'I have always been slow on the uptake so I was always left behind at school. The only teacher who ever put me on, she took about five of us in the evening, in her own time, unpaid in her own time, and she did more for us than any other teacher I ever came across' (Hull, 1997). With the Lifelong learning agenda, librarians are seen to be at centre stage as never before! Are we equal to the challenge? The position of power held by a teacher figure can also have very negative consequences if that power is abused when interacting with the more timid.

A 60-year-old, with a much lower than average reported self esteem rating, stated: 'When I went to school, you were frightened of the teachers. You didn't have a one-to-one relationship with them. If you didn't do right, you got a slap or something like that. It was the old ways' (Hull, 1997). Following a sympathetically delivered pre-retirement course, this student showed a large overall gain in her self-assessed self-esteem rating. The current ethos in teaching is ideally student-centred and takes account of the individual's strengths, weaknesses and preferred learning style. Librarians who teach should have some awareness of teaching methodology: happily, in UK university libraries at least, many of the librarians who currently deliver user education, do hold a teaching qualification.

I believe that images of librarians are changing, but change is slow. How much of the blame for negative images can be laid at the door of librarians themselves? When I changed track from being a lecturer in Adult Education, trained as a librarian and applied for a job in the public library service, at interview I was asked how I felt about 'leaving Education' and was greeted with bemusement when I replied that I did not consider that I had.

If we are honest with ourselves, we know that some of the old stereotypes were based on a grain of truth: as a child I certainly encountered the nit-picking public librarian dragon, as well as the kindly helpful one. The old dragons still have a lot to answer for. In the interests of eliminating any professional bias, I employed a non-librarian research assistant for the 'Barriers to Libraries Project' (Hull, 2000). She reported back that participants in focus groups, who had been interested enough in the project to take part, breathed a visible sigh of relief and became franker about gaps in their knowledge of things library-related as soon as she said that she wasn't a librarian herself. Why won't they tell *us*? Even by the 1990s all the dragons had not yet been slain.

Notes

1. St. Francis de Sales.
2. True art conceals the means by which it is achieved.

References

Adams, H. B. (1918) *The Education of Henry Adams*, Boston: Houghton Mifflin.

Angelou, M. (2002) *A Song Flung up to Heaven*, London: Virago.

Booth, A. and Brice, A. (2004) *Evidence Based Practice for Information Professionals: a handbook*, London: Facet Publishing.

Hughes, T. (1997) cited in Library and Information Commission (2000) *Libraries: The Essence of Inclusion*, London: Library and Information Commission.

Hull, B. (1997) 'Changes in the self concepts of adult students with special reference to previous educational disadvantage', University of Leeds (unpublished PhD).

Hull, B. (2000) 'Barriers to libraries as agents of lifelong learning', London: Library and Information Commission, available at *http://lis.tees.ac.uk/research/researchbh.cfm* (accessed 23/09/10).

'Image' (1985) 'How they're seeing us', *American Libraries*, December 1985.

'Image' (1986) 'How they're seeing us', *American Libraries*, July–August 1986.

Library and Information Commission (2000) *Libraries: the essence of inclusion*, London: Library and Information Commission.

McReynolds, R. (1985) 'A heritage dismissed', *Library Journal*, 110 (18), pp. 25–31.

Seale, M. (2008) 'Old maids, policemen, and social rejects: mass media representations and public perceptions of librarians', *Electronic Journal of Academic and Special Librarianship* 9, available at *http://southernlibrarianship. icaap.org/content/v09n01/seale_m01.html* (accessed 29/11/10).

4

Psychological barriers

Abstract: This chapter acts as a reminder of the psychological factors at play in all human interactions and how they can impact the accessibility of libraries and information. The problem of information overload is considered. Some suggestions are made as to how librarians can deal with the consequences of these phenomena.

Key words: losing face, human interactions, libraries, information overload, solutions.

Basic human psychology: anxiety

Typically, human beings have an in-built fear of the unknown and tend to be initially cautious in unfamiliar surroundings. The feeling of dread, experienced prior to entering a room full of strangers, is a common manifestation of this fear and the strength of feeling and the degree of ease with which it can be surmounted varies, depending on the psychological make-up of the individual. It is difficult for information professionals to imagine just how threatening a library environment can be to someone with little or no previous experience of a library: for them it is an unknown. This was already true when libraries were print-based; with the advent of electronic sources of information and the need for associated familiarity and skills the problem may well be compounded.

Mellon (1986) found that about 75 per cent of under-graduates experience some sort of anxiety when using the library, and that for the majority of students the transition from using a public library to using an academic library was a major one. 'Library anxiety' was the term used by Jiao and others (1996) to describe a psychological barrier and situation-specific anxiety, characterised by worry and emotionality. It manifests itself in tension, fear, negative self-defeating thoughts and mental disorganisation and leads to avoidance behaviour.

Losing face

Closely allied to the fear of the unknown is that of 'losing face', i.e. a threat towards a self image as competent and capable. To state it quite simply, nobody likes to look stupid! Michael Argyle has observed: 'Adolescents who have only just formed a tentative self image, are particularly sensitive to the reactions of others, and are insecure in this sense. People who have changed their social class, their job or their nationality are often in a similar position' (Argyle, 1972). This is borne out by the research done by Jiao and others (1996) which found that anxiety related to using an academic library was highest among young males, non-native speakers of English, those with high levels of academic achievement and those in full-time or part-time employment.

The pitfalls which may be present in unfamiliar surroundings offer multiple opportunities for perceived loss of face. The embarrassment felt is often irrational and out of proportion to the situation and can affect anyone and everyone; for example, in Italy, when attempting to send an e-mail in a hotel computer lounge, I discovered that the layout of the Italian keyboard is *different*; the @ symbol was nowhere to be found! Irrationally, this made me feel incredibly stupid and reminded me sharply of how naïve users must feel in unfamiliar surroundings.

Information providers should seek to make their public interfaces, human or electronic, as welcoming and non-threatening as possible. All possible steps should be taken to avoid putting the client into situations where he/she feels out of control or embarrassed. It has long been established that people do withdraw from situations that damage their self-image and seek interactions that confirm their self-image (Secord and Backman, 1964). Jiao and Onwuegbuzie (1999) found that the fear of negative social evaluation is an important antecedent of library anxiety. It is likely that students with low perceived social acceptance also tend to hold unrealistically high standards for themselves with respect to performing library tasks. Indeed, library anxious students tend to feel that other students are proficient at using the library, whereas they alone are incompetent, and that this incompetence is a source of embarrassment and consequently should be concealed. This desire to keep their perceived ineptness hidden leads to a reluctance to seek help from librarians for fear of having their perceived ignorance exposed (Mellon, 1988). Sometimes their discomfort is manifested in aggressive behaviour; more common is the avoidance of the location which causes them discomfort.

Kuhlthau (1991) attributes part of the discomfort and anxiety to the mismatch between how information providers arrange access to information and how the client conceptualises his/her information need: 'The cognitive and affective aspects of the process of information seeking suggest a gap between the users' natural process of information use and the information system and intermediaries' traditional patterns of information.' Although this was more applicable to traditional paper-based libraries and card catalogues (a book or card can only go in one place, notwithstanding added entries) it should be kept in mind that the information we offer only rarely fits the mindset of the enquirer perfectly. Each person is unique in how they perceive the world and, 'People actively and constantly construct their view of the world by assimilating and accommodating new information with what they already know or have experienced' (Kuhlthau, 1991). This seminal research led to the conclusion that the process of searching for information, whether the searcher is deemed to be a high achiever or not, is an anxiety producing process, which is assuaged when the information has been assimilated and incorporated into the information seeker's Weltanschauung.[1]

People engaged in professions which have a tradition of exuding confidence and control, e.g. lawyers and police officers, are often reluctant to display any sign of weakness, particularly in the presence of peers. For example, in the delivery of information handling sessions to groups of post graduate police inspectors, it was disquieting how few questions were asked in the group session: everything was evidently crystal clear. However, what was remarkable was the large number of individual students who returned later to ask in private the questions they were clearly afraid of asking in the presence of their peers.

User education sessions should perhaps give some recognition to the information seeking process, with its accompanying uncertainty at the outset, and an assurance of a greater feeling of certainty as the process evolves: 'Merely devising better means for orienting people to sources and technology, however, does not adequately address the issue of uncertainty and anxiety in the ISP' (Kuhlthau, 1991).

When addressing any group, where it is suspected that questions and discussions will be slow to fire up, it can be useful to have a 'plant' in the group to ask the first question. Most human beings are gregarious and will 'follow my leader'. I have put this theory to the test many times where I have been a member of an audience and asked the first question – which usually opens the gate for other questions. Quite often others tell me afterwards that they were hoping someone else would ask a question first, as they had thought that everyone else had understood everything fully.

People are human!

At every juncture information professionals should keep uppermost in their mind that people are only human, and will react in a human way in a situation where they do not feel at ease. How often do we find that the 'awkward customer' is someone who is perhaps not really conversant with how things work and fears exposure as ignorant or incompetent? How hard is it to resist the temptation to expose his incompetence to score a cheap victory! If we can control that natural urge and explain his misconceptions discreetly, he may well realise that we have guessed and may even appreciate our discretion and become an ally. In the past, having arrived in a new organisation and been pre-warned of such difficult people, it emerged that the 'awkward customer' persona was merely a mask for a lack of basic knowledge on how things work, e.g. the very senior academic who did not understand the principles of the Dewey system and wanted all 'his' books to be kept on one shelf in the library. Had his request been granted, resources related in a minor way to his main area of interest would have been inconveniently located for other users who had an interest in them. The longer the confrontation with the library went on, the more entrenched his views became until a new subject librarian was appointed who refused to accept the established view of him as an awkward customer, started with a clean slate and managed to subtly educate him on the vagaries of Dewey on the pretext of enlisting his help in educating the students. Some subject specialist lecturers or teachers are not as up to date as librarians on library and information matters and why should they be? It's not their specialism! However, some do see this as a sign of failure, and are afraid that their students who attend the latest library instruction sessions may end up knowing more than they do – leaving them with a feeling of being no longer 'in charge'. No lecturer wants to be contradicted by a smart-ass 'barrack room lawyer' student. As librarians we must recognise this phenomenon and ensure that lecturers have lots of opportunities to update their information skills. This may be achieved in a variety of ways: offering lecturers private, one-to-one, tailored updating sessions; inviting them to be present when the student sessions are delivered; involving them in the preparation of the teaching materials used in the sessions. Besides having the great educational benefit of firmly embedding information literacy skills, these activities serve to protect the ego of lecturers and build stronger links and allies.

Information overload

A more general problem, not confined to interacting with libraries and librarians, and which came very much to the fore with the proliferation of information made possible through the Internet, is that commonly known as 'information overload' – which has been cited as causing multiple problems for many professionals and managers; it is reported that 'in a survey sponsored by Reuters International, 1,300 managers in Hong Kong, Singapore, the UK, and the US reported that while they needed lots of information to perform effectively, 25 per cent of them also suffer ill health, ranging from headaches to depression, as a direct result of the enormous amount of information they have to absorb' (Farhoomand and Drury, 2002).

The same feeling of being overwhelmed by the volume of information/misinformation can strike when a Google search is performed by the informationally naïve: the resulting 30,000 hits can create feelings of inadequacy and even a shadow of the sorcerer's apprentice's fear, 'Die Geister, die ich rief',[2] summoning help that cannot be subsequently controlled.

The phenomenon of an embarrassment of information has been dubbed 'infobesity' and, as Bawden and Robinson (2008) state, is far from new: 'The writer of Ecclesiastes, who remarked that "of making many books there is no end; and much study is a weariness of the flesh" (ch 12, v 6), was the first of a long line of commentators who saw the proliferation of information as a detriment to effectiveness and efficiency.'

The panic at being presented with so much information is similar to that experienced by a first-time visitor to the Louvre, especially one who has previously been told that if a visitor were to spend just 30 seconds looking at each of the 35,000 items, and even without allowing time for a break or for movement between exhibits, the visit would last over 12 days. Depending on their personality type, some visitors find this information daunting to the point of ruining their visit. If someone else can succeed in getting them to focus on the type of art which interests them most and to view that, or even to point out that most first-time non-specialist visitors tend to 'scalp hunt' the Mona Lisa, the Venus de Milo and the Virgin of the Rocks to start with, they will probably feel less panicky. This is not unlike the intervention of a good librarian who can help those suffering from the overload produced by Google by getting them first to focus on what they really want, construct their search strategy and evaluate the results. The Internet has been marketed as easy to use, and so it is, but it still needs information handling skills to maximise its use. Who better to impart these skills than an understanding librarian?

Notes

1. View of the world.
2. 'The spirits that I summoned'.

References

Argyle, M. (1972) *The Psychology of Interpersonal Behaviour*, 2nd edn, Harmondsworth: Penguin.

Bawden, D. and Robinson, L. (2009) 'The dark side of information: overload, anxiety and other paradoxes and pathologies', *Journal of Information Science*, 35(2), pp. 180–91.

Farhoomand, A.F. and Drury, D.H. (2002) 'Managerial information overload', *Communications of the ACM*, 45, 10, pp. 127–31.

Jiao, Q.G. and others (1996) 'Library anxiety: characteristics of "At risk" college students', *Library and Information Science Research*, 18, Spring 1996.

Jiao, Q.G. and Onwuegbuzie, A.J. (1999) 'Self-perception and library anxiety: an empirical study', *Library Review*, 48(3), pp. 140–7.

Kuhlthau, C.C. (1991) 'Inside the search process: information seeking from the user's perspective', *Journal of the*

American Society for Information Science, 42(5), pp. 361–71.

Mellon, C.A. (1986) 'Library anxiety: a grounded theory and its development', *College and Research Libraries*, March 1986.

Mellon, C.A. (1988) 'Attitudes: the forgotten dimension in library instruction', *Library Journal*, Vol. 113, pp. 137–9.

Secord, P.F. and Backman, C.W. (1964) *Social Psychology*, New York: McGraw-Hill.

5

Social class and lack of education as barriers

Abstract: This chapter examines social class and low levels of education as barriers to library access. The degree to which the establishment perpetuates the status quo is considered and the important role of individual library staff members in assisting the possible social progression of individual clients is examined.

Key words: social class, social progression, establishment attitudes, role of library staff.

Social class and education

The centrality of a library in true education has long been acknowledged: 'The true University of these days is a collection of books' (Carlyle). 'A university is just a group of buildings gathered around a library' (Foote).

The connection between social class and educational achievement has been well documented for many years. Many would argue that in a democracy, participation in education should offer an opportunity to improve one's lot both in terms of income and to enhance one's perceived status by changing social class. In a democracy this is theoretically possible and some individuals are able to realise their ambitions by this route. Sadly, however, the educational system often serves to support the status quo and reinforce the class barriers it could help to demolish. It is interesting that in 2000, the following appeared in the Harvard Educational Review when re-issuing a report of classic research conducted in the US:

> In 1970 the *Harvard Educational Review* published an article by Ray Rist that described how, for the one class of children he observed, their public school not only mirrored the class system of the larger society but also actively contributed to maintaining it. Now, thirty years later, the Editorial Board of the *Harvard Educational Review* has decided to reprint this article as part of the HER Classics Series. We hope that by reacquainting readers with this article, and by introducing it to new readers, we can encourage all of us to think about the work that remains in creating a just and equitable educational experience for all children. (Rist, 2000)

In the traditionally class-ridden society of the UK we learn:

> All the independent evidence shows overall standards to be rising. But the bad news is that when it comes to the link between educational achievement and social class, Britain is at the bottom of the league for industrialised countries ... We continue to have one of the greatest class divides in education in the industrialised world, with a socio-economic attainment gap evident in children as young as 22 months ... Today, three-quarters of young people born into the top social class get five or more good GCSEs, but the figure for those born at the bottom is less than one-third ... Four factors are key to this depressing pattern. First the simple fact of growing up in poverty, with the restrictions it places on housing, diet and lifestyle. Second, family factors –

critically parental interest and support, which itself is driven by parental experience of education. Third, neighbourhood factors. The fourth is the quality of schooling. The first three require long-term change in social and economic life. But the great power of schooling is that it is in our power to change it now and change it for the better. (Miliband, 2003)

A survey of more than 2,000 pupils in Nottinghamshire concluded that educational attainment reflects the social class background of the pupils. Using a points system based on GCSE grades, the pupils of parents with manual jobs averaged 18.5 points; those from clerical backgrounds averaged 29.2; and those from a professional background averaged 41.7 points (Social class and educational performance, 1993).

As was argued in Chapter 2 the take up of public library services is, at least in the UK, historically linked to social class. Given the role of the public libraries in the rollout of ICT services, any lack of synergy between the library and a disadvantaged social group can only compound that disadvantage.

Libraries' potential for social engineering

Public library staff are part of the problem rather than the solution. With the exception of some notable individuals and authorities, the service is managed and operated by middle class people who share their middle class values with middle class library users. This makes the system self perpetuating and has marginalised all previous attempts to tackle social exclusion, such as

community librarianship. Public libraries have institutionalised classism, which is a reflection of a societal
problem, in the same way that institutionalised racism
has been recognised in the police force. (Pateman, 1999)

Research on the potentially transformative role of the
public library in underprivileged areas in France makes
informative and inspiring reading. Petit (1998) quotes 24-
year-old Daoud:

> When you're in the suburbs, you're supposed to do
> badly at school and get a lousy job, everything pushes
> you in that direction. I was able to dodge and avoid
> that path, to be different, to go somewhere else, that is
> where I belong. Those who just hang out, they do what
> society expects them to do, that's all. They're violent,
> they're vulgar, they're uneducated. They say : 'I live in
> the suburbs, and this is what I am.' I was just like them.
> Going to libraries like this one enabled me to have an
> access and to meet other people. That's what libraries
> are for. I chose my life and they didn't.

Here when he speaks of 'dodging' he means escaping the
well-trodden path that starts with education and training
that yield minimal qualifications and lead to unemployment
and failure. Sadly, Petit acknowledged that the young people
he met during his research weren't very 'representative' but
optimistically adds:

> In those places where librarians have been reflecting
> since many years on their role towards this 'public', it is
> an increasing proportion of the population that is
> taking over the libraries and their contents in order to
> outsmart the laws of 'social reproduction' and resist

exclusion, thus building their participation in a civil society. (Petit, 1998)

A cautionary note

This kind of compensatory force made possible by committed librarians, thankfully, continues but any expectation of a great reversal of existing trends of library use would be unrealistic. Single-handed, librarians cannot change the world but can often make a powerful contribution to those who have chosen to change. One of the salient points of the above example is that Daoud himself made the initial decision to improve his situation. As experienced teachers know, there is an optimum moment for any learner, either child or adult, when they are *receptive* to what is on offer – the state commonly referred to as 'readiness to learn'. In children this is dependent largely on cognitive development. In adults this is shaped by other factors:

> From the perspective of individual consciousness and activity, adults' readiness to learn can partly be understood in terms of Bourdieu's concept of habitus. The latter is a system of dispositions that allows and governs how a person acts, thinks and orients him/herself in the social world. This system of dispositions is a result of social experiences, collective memories and ways of thinking that have been engraved in the mind. Bourdieu's theory rests on the idea that habitus, formed by the life they have lived, govern individuals conceptions and practice and in this way contribute to the reproduction of the social world and sometimes – in the occurrence of lacking agreement between habitus and the social world – to change. (Rubenson, 2000)

In describing the project which had been of such great benefit to Daoud, Petit (1998) also refers to other young people in the area who used their contact with the library to perpetrate acts of disruption and vandalism. He concludes that their behaviour was an attack on what they viewed as a representative of the system that had failed them. This may be so, but librarians, or indeed anyone, working in what are often termed 'challenging' areas, should not tolerate such disruption for various reasons: first everyone (including librarians), deserves to be treated with respect; second, if the miscreants are allowed to run riot it will not advance their own self development and they are clearly not 'ready to learn'; finally, and most importantly, it will ruin the chances of those at whom the outreach is aimed – those who are 'ready to learn'. Librarians who work in such areas are normally aware of the personal qualities needed and recognise when the moment is not right; one librarian recounting her experiences on a 'rough' estate in the urban wastelands of northern England, explained: 'I had to send for the police quite regularly because there were kids climbing all over the library roof. But it wasn't bad - there were a *few* you knew you were getting through to.'

In the UK, Book Marketing Limited (1995) found that ownership of a library ticket increased with social class.[1] As many as 72 per cent of ABs had a library ticket as did 66 per cent of C1s. But only 52 per cent of C2s had a ticket and this figure fell to 47 per cent for DEs. England and Sumsion (1995) found that 54 per cent of library users from social class AB and 59 per cent of C1s used a public library at least once a month, but only 42 per cent of class C2 and 44 per cent of users in social class DE made the same journey. The proportion of non-users among the working class was also high, especially among DEs – and this trend was more marked in 1995 than in 1989. Middle-class users were more likely to borrow non-fiction books, use the reservation service and take advantage of non-borrowing library facilities.

Much of the research undertaken on social class has been in relation to public libraries, given that more individuals will come into contact with the public library than any other. However, it would be a mistake to conclude that these findings are only of interest to public librarians. For many individuals, their perception of libraries as a whole is strongly coloured by their experiences, positive or negative, with the public library sector. Research commissioned by the Library and Information Commission reports on students' attitudes to using College and University libraries being coloured by their early contacts with the public library service:

> For many, their first library experience had been with the Public Library Service which produced both positive and negative observations. Many report being been taken to the Public Library at an early age and there is evidence of good practice by these Public Libraries: 'My father used to go regularly every week so I used to go with him. The staff made you feel very welcome' (student aged over 40).

> The value of being introduced to Libraries at an early age was recognised by those who had had this experience: 'If your parents are saying "It's a good thing to read," that's good. It makes it a lot easier when you get older to do things off your own bat' (Social Sciences student, aged under 21).

> Although most reports of Public Library use were positive, the importance of appropriate personal

qualities of those dealing with customers should not be under-estimated. Just as memories of positive encounters remain, so do those of negative ones: 'I remember particularly one librarian who everybody commented on. She was the most sour-faced unfriendly woman on the face of the planet. If you wanted to take a book out, it was like you had committed a mortal sin!' (Social Sciences student, aged under 21). (Hull, 2000)

Let's hope this librarian retired years ago. My personal childhood memories of using the public library in a very working class area of Manchester are much more positive: I do remember the librarians as kind, gentle and helpful but also that we were all rather in awe of them as they sounded 'posh' – the classic gulf between the classes. I am very glad that they did not 'dumb down' in an attempt to accommodate their working class clientele. What they did do was to be patient, kind and accessible and to provide an organised access to knowledge and entertainment for those who were motivated to seek it; I remain eternally grateful to these librarians at Dickinson Road Library (now closed). Like a good teacher, a good librarian 'effects eternity; he can never know where his influence stops' (Adams, 1918).

Librarians cannot transform society single handed, but what they can do is lend a helping hand to those who may be on a journey of self transformation.

Note

1. Classes AB being professional and supervisory classes; C1 and C2 clerical and skilled manual workers; D semi-skilled workers; E unskilled workers or unemployed.

References

Adams, H.B. (1918) *The Education of Henry Adams*, Boston: Houghton Mifflin.

Book Marketing Limited (1995) *Books and the Consumer*, London: BML.

Carlyle, T. (n.d.) 'The hero as man of letters', *On Heroes and Hero Worship*, London: J.M. Dent & Sons, cited in *http://archive.ifla.org/I/humour/subj.htm* (accessed 13/10/10).

England, L. and Sumsion, J. (1995) 'Perspectives of public library use', Loughborough: Library and Information Statistics Unit, Department of Information and Library Studies, Loughborough University.

Foote, S. (n.d.) cited in *http://archive.ifla.org/I/humour/subj .htm* (accessed 13/10/10).

Hull, B. (2000) 'Barriers to Libraries as agents of lifelong learning', London: Library and Information Commission, available at *http://lis.tees.ac.uk/research/researchbh.cfm* (accessed 23/09/10).

Miliband, D. (2003) from a speech in Newcastle by the schools minister to an IPPR conference on social mobility, *Independent*, 8 September 2003.

Pateman, J. (1999) *Public libraries and social class*, Public Library Policy and Social Exclusion Working Paper 3, Leeds: Department of Information Management, Leeds Metropolitan University.

Petit, M. (1998) 'From libraries to citizenship: Study on young users in low-income neighborhoods of French cities', Paper presented at 64th IFLA General Conference, 16–21 August 1998, available at *http://archive.ifla.org/IV/ ifla64/078-155e.htm* (accessed 1/12/10).

Rist, R. (2000) 'HER classic reprint – student social class and teacher expectations: The self-fulfilling prophecy in ghetto education', *Harvard Educational Review*, 70(3) Fall 2000, pp. 257–405.

Rubenson, K. (2000) 'Adults' readiness to learn: Questioning lifelong learning for all', available at *www.aare.edu .au/00pap/rub00473.htm* (accessed 25/01/11).

Social class and educational performance (1993) *Sociology Update*, 1993.

6

Language as a barrier

Abstract: This chapter examines the global domination of the English language and the concept of, sometimes unintended, linguistic imperialism. It shows that language is not the only problem facing non-native students.

Key words: English for speakers of other languages, linguistic imperialism, cultural differences.

Predominance of English as a world language

The key role played by the English language as a tool of international communication is not in dispute: 'The British Empire may be in full retreat with the handover of Hong Kong. But from Bengal to Belize and Las Vegas to Lahore, the language of the sceptred isle is rapidly becoming the first global lingua franca' (Globe and Mail, 1997) is perhaps a rather simplistic account of a more complex phenomenon. The influence of English in the world, although once attributable to the might of the British Empire, probably owes most nowadays to the economic influence of the anglophone USA and the spread of the Internet. Chinese, not English, is the language spoken by the greatest *number* of people in the world but English is unique in that its use is widespread across the globe. Crystal (2003) dubs this 'a unique event', with over 329 million using English as their first language and a further 430 million as a second language, an event without precedent, unless we count the spread of Latin via the Roman Empire – when the world was a much smaller place.

Psychological problems of English language predominance

For those who speak English as a second language, and especially those who are educated in English, there can be psychological repercussions. The fact that English is the medium may be perceived, albeit subconsciously, as an *elevation* of English, with a corresponding perceived or implied devaluation of the mother tongue. Why are the French so reluctant to speak in English? One reason, according to Dr Bhaskaran Nayar, is that if you talk in another person's language, then you are surrendering a bit of power (*Guardian*, 15 June 2004). The concept of 'linguistic imperialism' has been suggested, with a tendency 'to see the English language as a means of communicating a whole value system' with an 'us and them attitude' – a mild patronisation. The British and Americans are notoriously poor learners of other languages, often claiming that wherever one travels in the world, there will always be someone who speaks English, often said with a swagger, implying the innate superiority of their mother tongue. Linguistic imperialism may be deduced from the American Embassy statement, 'Trade follows the book'; there are indeed vested interests in making English the world's lingua franca, as it has always been seen as virtually impossible to learn a culture-free language. 'Langue et Civilisation' is a well established principle in language teaching. Crystal (2003), however, argues that 'English is now so widely established that it can no longer be thought of as owned by one nation'. Is it possible for assumed cultural norms to be separated from the use of English in a given situation, such as the delivery of a programme of study in Higher Education? Could those responsible for the delivery of the programme be seen as guilty, even unwittingly, of linguistic imperialism?

The number of non-native speakers of English in British universities continues to grow, but there are some indications that this situation is not without problems.

Studying in Higher Education in English

A 2005 British Government initiative to reveal previously secret examiners' reports brought to light the fact that there are 'concerns about [among other issues] the poor grasp of English by overseas students ... [the Vice chancellor of a northern university] confirmed his fears that the website would "dish the dirt around the international stage" and unfairly damage reputations – and even Britain's position in the international market' (*Times Higher*, 25 March 2005).

Apart from purely language difficulties, many overseas students report feeling isolated in the UK. 'International students find it tough to make UK friends, and many are put off socialising by the heavy drinking culture and "smugness and superiority" of British people, according to a survey published this week' (*Times Higher*, 3 December 2004). According to the 2004 UKCOSA report referred to, nearly three quarters of postgraduate and more than half of undergraduate international students said they had no UK friends. UK students were considered hard to get to know by 43 per cent, and more than half felt that making contact with

British people outside their institution was difficult (*Times Higher*, 3 December 2004). Given that informal interactions outside the classroom provide a potentially key element in language acquisition, these reports should perhaps be cause for concern. The situation is not new; in a UK COSA review of unpublished research (Leonard, Pelletier and Morley, 2003) problems with language figure specifically on a regular basis. Here is a selection of the problems mentioned:

Language in particular is cited as 'the most common explanation for academic failure' in the report of Makepeace and Baxter (1990). Jin (1992) highlighted the experiences of Chinese students in the UK and remarked on the mutual lack of understanding of the other's academic culture by both UK lecturers and Chinese students, and concluded, inter alia, 'the higher the Chinese students competence in language, without understanding the target British cultural discourse, the greater the problems'. The cultural aspects of communication are highlighted in Yeh (2001), who reports that, although postgraduate international students are expected to be able to talk 'appropriately', they may not have developed the skills involved in communicating effectively across cultures.

Unsatisfactory practices in dealing with international students were highlighted by the publication of external examiners reports by the Quality Assurance Agency for Higher Education. 'The Times Higher analysed hundreds of reports from external examiners [which] reveal concerns [including] poor grasp of English by overseas students and the need for remedial support for weak students' (*Times Higher*, 25 March 2005).

Many UK institutions receive students from all over the world. Additionally, undergraduates come on short (one semester) exchange schemes from the European Union; other EU students spend one year at a university as part of joint degree schemes between their home university and the one in the UK.

Through teaching English to some of these students I have been able to gain some insights into the reception they feel they have had from university staff and other students. What is noticeable to an onlooker is that international students tend to socialise among themselves, and not necessarily just by shared language and nationality, but rather as a 'non-English' entity. The Spanish are more likely to be friends with the Libyans, French or Germans than with their English fellow students. Some *do* make English friends, but they are a minority; a number say the English students they share accommodation with are impatient with their relative lack of skills in English and are unwilling to make any allowances. They report little criticism of lecturing staff, but sometimes feel left out of jokes made by lecturers which are only accessible to native speakers!

Difficulties with accents

Other informal research undertaken with lecturing staff indicates that some concessions *are* indeed made in dealing with overseas students' written work, but often it is in oral situations that problems can arise. Admitting that he himself was not an 'English specialist', one course leader interviewed showed little awareness of the problems caused by regional accents, amazed that anyone who had learnt English could not take a Liverpudlian or Scottish accent in their stride (Hull, 2009). Regional accents in the UK, or indeed anywhere, can present great problems for foreign learners who have only been taught 'Received Pronunciation' (although less than 3 per cent of the population actually speak it). I well remember a French colleague, a lecturer *in*

English at a French University who spoke perfect Received Pronunciation, and failed miserably to aurally decipher the Manchester accent, as spoken by over 2.5 million English native speakers! We should therefore recognise that learning a foreign language sufficiently well to function on a day to day basis in a foreign country is no mean feat: anyone who has experienced this for themselves will recall the sheer exhaustion of straining to follow what is going on and responding appropriately before the native speakers have moved on and changed the subject completely, as is normal in the nature of human conversation. But native speakers of English are notoriously poor students of other languages: why bother? There is always someone who speaks English, isn't there?

It is clear that, although it is non-intentional, there is some evidence of a lack of sensitivity vis-à-vis language use when dealing with international students.

However, even more important is the different educational ethos of the UK and other countries in the developed world. For many of our overseas students the shock of not receiving ready-packaged pearls of wisdom from the teacher is world shattering.

Gu (2009) quotes from the observations of a postgraduate Chinese student:

> When I first started my MA, I felt very strongly that I was not used to the teaching and learning environment at all. . . . The teaching style was very different from that in China. Chinese students were taught like stuffed ducks in China, while here students are encouraged to take part in group discussions. . . . I also found that language could be a barrier, particularly in listening. I could not quite understand students from countries like Malaysia. A particular teacher had a very strong local

accent, which I could hardly understand. (Zhang, male, Postgraduate Student)

The problems experienced by the students are also noted by their tutors. A postgraduate lecturer observes:

> Yes, they have serious difficulty adjusting to expectations of the British education system. ... We are trying to encourage an autonomous approach to study ... Understanding that difference [in teaching] is extremely challenging to learners when they come on the course, because they are expecting to be told what to learn, what to read, the answers to produce, and they are ready to work hard doing that ... Some students welcome that. Some students are worried, intimidated, confused by that shift of responsibility ... Yes, the language can be a problem. But I think cultural issues are far more important. (Gu, 2009)

Cultural differences

When the cultural dimensions of Hofstede (1986) are applied to teaching and learning, it may be observed that in collective societies, like China, students are expected to learn 'how to do', while in individualist societies like the UK, students are expected to learn 'how to learn'.

The way societies differ from each other has been analysed using a number of parameters; one analysis by Hofstede uses, among others, the notion of a 'power distance index' which is the extent to which the less powerful members of organisations and institutions (like the family) accept and expect that power is distributed unequally. This represents inequality (more versus less), but defined from below, not from above. It suggests that a society's level of inequality is endorsed by the followers as much as by the leaders. Power and inequality, of course, are extremely fundamental facts of any society and anybody with some international experience will be aware that 'all societies are unequal, but some are more unequal than others' (Hofstede, 2010).

Table 6.1 (Hofstede, 1986, p. 313) shows the different expectations of teachers and students in different power distance societies, which point to the important role of culture in the formation of teaching and learning traditions.

From a practical point of view, these ideas are very important for librarians in educational establishments: if overseas students have not been previously taught in an atmosphere which requires them to conduct their own research and arrive at their own conclusions, they are less likely to have the necessary skills to conceptualise and conduct effective literature searches and to apply the necessary degree of discernment in sifting the results of a search. In a small research project of a sample of 400+ students of 36 nationalities (of which 31 per cent were Chinese) 46 per cent were not familiar with using journals.

Table 6.1	Large/small power distance societies and teaching and learning cultures
Large power distance societies	**Small power distance societies**
a teacher merits the respect of his/her students (Confucius)	a teacher should respect the independence of his/her students
teacher-centred education	student-centred education
students expect teacher to initiate communication	teacher expects students to initiate communication
students speak up in class only when invited by the teacher	students may speak up spontaneously in class
effectiveness of learning related to excellence of the teacher	effectiveness of learning related to amount of two-way communication in class

Plagiarism is a general problem in higher education, but particularly with students from other cultures: 23 per cent of the same sample said that in their home country, they were allowed to use the words of others without referencing.

Similar differences emerged with teaching and assessment methods: 55 per cent had no experience of doing individual presentations and 47 per cent had not even done a group presentation (Hull, 2010). It is not difficult to imagine the added tension, if the student is expected to acquire and demonstrate these skills in, what for them, is a foreign language.

Overseas students, therefore, besides having the extra burden of having to function and study in a foreign language, are less likely than home students to have any existing knowledge on, inter alia, literature searching, referencing, and the concept of plagiarism. The library can show sensitivity in dealing with non-native speakers, by remembering to speak clearly and avoiding regionalisms and colloquialisms. It may be appropriate to have special events or services for non-native speakers. An interesting example of good practice, to ease the initial transition to studying completely in English, is the use of recorded library tours in Arabic, Mandarin Chinese and French at the University of Birmingham in the UK (see *www.library.bham. ac.uk/searching/infoskills/french_mainlibrary_audiotours. shtml* (accessed 3/12/10)). This is not a cheap project to undertake and might not be appropriate in some libraries. It is noteworthy because it demonstrates a degree of under-standing of the difficulties of studying in an all-English environment and offers an opportunity to get started with a clear understanding of a key service.

References

Crystal, D. (2003) *English as a Global Language*, 2nd edn, Cambridge: Cambridge University Press.

Globe and Mail, Toronto, 12 July 1997 (cited in Crystal, 2003).

Gu, Q. (2009) 'Maturity and Interculturality: Chinese students' experiences in UK higher education', *European Journal of Education*, Vol. 44, No. 1, 2009, Part 1.

Guardian, 15 June 2004, 'Work in progress: Does being a teacher of English give you power over your foreign pupils?'.

Hofstede, G. (1986) 'Cultural differences in teaching and learning', *International Journal of Intercultural Relations*, 10, pp. 301–320.

Hofstede, G. (2010) *Cultural Dimensions, www.geert-hofstede.com/* (accessed 9 /11/10).

Hull, B. (2000) 'Barriers to Libraries as agents of lifelong learning', London: Library and Information Commission, available at *http://lis.tees.ac.uk/research/researchbh.cfm* (accessed 23/09/10).

Hull, B. (2009) Unpublished research at Teesside University, UK.

Hull, B. (2010) Unpublished research at Teesside University, UK.

Jin, L. (1992) 'Academic cultural expectations and second language use: Chinese postgraduate students in the UK – a cultural synergy model', PhD Thesis, University of Leicester.

Leonard, D., Pelletier, C. and Morley, L. (2003) 'The experiences of international students in UK Higher Education: a review of unpublished research', London: UKCOSA. The Council for International Education.

Makepeace, E. and Baxter, A. (1990) 'Overseas students and academic failure: a national study', *Journal of International Education*, 1, 1.

Sovics, S. (2008) 'The International Students' Experience Project. Creative Learning in Practice', Centre for Excellence in Teaching and Learning.

Times Higher, 3 December 2004, 'UK mores alienate foreign students'.

Times Higher, 25 March 2005, 'Official reports "dish the dirt"'.

Yeh, C. Y. (2001) 'Socio-cultural awareness and cross-cultural first encounters', PhD thesis, University of Newcastle-upon-Tyne.

7

Lack of literacy and numeracy skills as a barrier

Abstract: This chapter examines the problems of low literacy and numeracy skills, how this can interfere with access to information and why information providers need to be aware of these potential problems.

Key words: low literacy, low numeracy, information systems, awareness of information professionals.

Varying levels of literacy and numeracy

In any human interaction there are often assumptions made about basic underlying life knowledge, skills, and the subtext. There are certain 'givens' which do not need to be explicit every time an interaction between two individuals from the same social group takes place; this frequently leads to communication which is almost telegraphic in style and which uses the jargon of the group. Problems only arise when the attempted communication is with a non group member. Librarians and other professionals are usually well educated, often middle class, and used to communicating with those of similar backgrounds; such communication is based on the existence of certain knowledge and skills. There already exists a certain degree of sensitivity in using plain words in communication intended for a wide audience; e.g., the Plain English Campaign (Plain English, 2011) has been battling against jargon and gobbledegook since 1979. Nevertheless, assumptions can still unwittingly occur – made by one of the most literate professions: that everyone else shares the same level of literacy and numeracy skills. By way of illustration: in the late 1970s a young, impecunious, unemployed librarian in the UK registered with a temping agency for office work and, as an applicant for office work in those pre-computerised days, as part of the recruitment process was given a series of filing tests, putting things in order, alphabetical and numerical; she amazed the agency by completing the tests in record time and with 100 per cent accuracy as apparently this had never happened before during recruitment testing. But anybody could do this, she thought, surely these skills are almost second nature? On reflection, yes they are (or were), to *librarians*. But 'normal' people do have strange gaps. Many years after the temping job, that same librarian was greeted with disbelief when, at an information professionals' conference, she reported research on university students who did not understand decimals and could not easily recite the alphabet, *although they were not illiterate or innumerate in the narrow sense of the word.*

The alphabet and related problems

It was interesting to read the following in a recent novel: 'Ben never went to school but his father had a huge library and so he was immensely well read. When he went to university he discovered that he had read everything on the reading list for the 3 year course by the time he was 12, but he didn't know the order of the letters in the alphabet or the months of the year' (Stevenson, 2002).

However, the evidence on literacy and numeracy difficulties is not merely anecdotal; the Moser Report (Moser, 1999) reported that 7 million adults (one in five) in England are functionally illiterate. This means that if they were given the Yellow pages telephone directory, they could not find the page number for 'Plumbers'. Table 7.1 indicates that the problem is not confined to Britain.

These percentages relate to level 1 as defined in the International Adult Literacy Survey (OECD).

Many other people, often well educated and far from illiterate, have problems with spelling. They often experience great frustration when using information systems which demand perfect spelling and particular punctuation, e.g. a system which demands 'Dickens, C' (Dickens comma space C) and will not retrieve anything if the enquirer types 'C Dickens'.

Additionally, many people who are far from illiterate do not use alphabetical and numerical sequences with the same accuracy and regularity as librarians; e.g., on the 'Who wants to be a millionaire?' quiz show, some contestants on the tie-breaker actually fail completely to put just 4 items into alphabetical order. I am told by a friend, who interviews for British Government surveys, that when she presents interviewees with an alphabetically-arranged stack of stimulus cards and, during the course of the interview, asks them to turn to card 'n', they frequently do not have the skills to find card 'n' and look through the cards from the

Table 7.1	Percentage of adults with low literacy and low numeracy	
	Literacy	Numeracy
Germany	12%	7%
Canada	17%	17%
Britain	23%	23%

beginning, a, b, c, d etc, until they come to card 'n'. Am I suggesting that we librarians teach our clients alphabetical order? No, of course not, but it is important to be sensitive to possible weaknesses.

Definition of literacy

It is perhaps useful to reflect on what is meant by 'literacy'. This is the OECD definition:

> Many previous studies have treated literacy as a condition that adults either have or do not have. The IALS (The International Adult Literacy Survey) no longer defines literacy in terms of an arbitrary standard of reading performance, distinguishing the few who completely fail the test (the 'illiterates') from nearly all those growing up in OECD countries who reach a minimum threshold (those who are 'literate'). Rather, proficiency levels along a continuum denote how well adults use information to function in society and the economy. Thus, literacy is defined as a particular capacity and mode of behaviour: the ability to understand and employ printed information in daily activities, at home, at work and in the community, in order to achieve one's goals, and to develop one's knowledge and potential. Differences in levels of literacy matter both economically and socially: literacy affects, inter alia, labour quality and flexibility, employment, training opportunities, income from work and wider participation in civic society ... Literacy is defined as a particular capacity and mode of behaviour, the ability to understand and employ printed information in daily activities, at home, at work and in

the community – to achieve one's goals, and to develop one's knowledge and potential. (OECD, 2000)

Problems with decimals

The Dewey Decimal classification scheme can also cause considerable consternation; many people simply do not understand decimals as a filing system. In interviews for the Barriers to Libraries Project (Hull, 2000) a number expressed feeling inadequate because of their failure to understand the Decimal Classification system and the floor layouts on sequences of books. 'The only problem is finding books. It's the codes on the end. It's when you get to the little extensions on the end that I have trouble'. (Male student, Software Engineering, aged 19–21)

Not long ago, a student nurse asked me to go to the shelves with her to find a book of which the catalogue indicated 6 copies available. They were all there, in the correct sequence, which I took the opportunity of explaining to her as gently as possible. As she thanked me she explained that in the past when she could not find books on the shelf, she had gone out and bought them. Why had she not asked before? Like many users, she felt that she ought to know how to find books and her inability to do so was a sign of failure.

Unfortunately, for the UK at least, things are not improving on reading and mathematical skills: figures from the OECD, measured over the six years to 2006, showed that mathematics standards among 15-year-olds have plummeted, with 16 countries overtaking Britain since 2000, including Slovenia, Belgium, the Netherlands, Denmark and Austria. The UK also fell from 8th to 24th place in the international league table. Standards in reading also declined, with the UK falling behind 10 countries, among them Poland, Sweden, the

Netherlands and Japan. Britain fell from 7th to 17th place (PISA, 2006). So, the future is not necessarily brighter.

Falling statistics for enquiries

Somewhat disquieting is the report that the number of enquiries in university libraries is falling. Enquiries per FTE equivalent fell over 10 years to 2004 by 43 per cent for 'new' UK universities and 10.5 for 'old' universities (Table 3.18, LISU, 2006). 'The reasons for this can only be a matter for speculation. Suggestions include changes in the layout of library buildings leading to increased user independence in being able to locate resources for themselves; increasing familiarity with availability of electronic resources leading enquirers to look elsewhere before asking the library; and the position and staffing of enquiry desks within the library or at joint enquiry points with other services' (LISU, 2006).

Could any of the fall in the number of enquiries and numbers of books issued be attributable to the clients' inability to penetrate the sometimes arcane shelving systems and taking the line of least resistance and 'Googling it', regardless of the reliability of the information retrieved? None of us likes to lose face: interviews in the Barriers to Libraries Project (Hull, 2000) revealed over and over again that the failure to ask for help was dictated by the belief that everyone else knew what they were doing and one's own inability was a sign of inadequacy. Particularly poignant were the comments from a 41-year-old man, made unemployed by the closure of the local steel works, who was enrolled on a government-funded New Deal course:

> I wasn't given a tour to start off with. A lot of it is which floor you need to be on. For someone who has

never been in a library, let alone a University Library, it can be fairly intimidating. ... I can get by without using it. It's optional in my point of view. If I had been given a tour maybe some of the fears may have been diminished. I have had problems. I gave it up as a bad job. (Hull, 2000)

The course organisers had obviously not considered whether the course participants had the necessary information retrieval skills, and had not arranged an induction session before sending them to the library. Here was a missed opportunity for possible enrichment of an individual's life experiences and a clear example of lack of liaison between course leader and library. Communication is indeed the issue!

Closely linked to literacy and numeracy, and dependent on them, is the ability to access information and communication technology – which is the subject of the next chapter.

References

Hull, B. (2000) 'Barriers to Libraries as agents of lifelong learning', London: Library and Information Commission, available at *http://lis.tees.ac.uk/research/researchbh.cfm* (accessed 23/09/10).

LISU (2006), *Annual Library Statistics,* available at *www.lboro.ac.uk/departments/dils/lisu/pages/publications/als06.html* (accessed 23/08/10).

Moser, C. (1999) 'A fresh start. Improving literacy and numeracy', Report of the working group chaired by Sir Claus Moser. UK Department for Education and Employment.

OECD (2000) 'Literacy in the information age. Final report of the adult literacy survey', OECD Publishing. Available from: *www.oecd.org/document/2/0,3343,en_2649_39263 294_2670850_1_1_1_1,00.html* (accessed 16 /9/10).

PISA (2006) 'Executive Summary PISA, Science Competencies for Tomorrow's World', OECD, available at *www.pisa .oecd.org/dataoecd/15/13/39725224.pdf* (accessed 22/8/10).

Plain English Campaign (2011) *www.plainenglish.co.uk/* (accessed 4/01/11).

Stevenson, H. (2002) *Instructions for visitors*, London: Black Swan, p. 65.

8

Information and Communication Technology as a barrier

Abstract: This chapter considers human–computer interactions, some changes resulting from technological advances, computer phobias and frustrations and the continued existence of the digital divide.

Key words: human–computer interactions, computer phobia, computer frustrations, digital divide.

Difficulties with using ICT to access information may be seen as falling into two main categories: first there are the phobias and frustrations in human–computer interactions experienced by those who are familiar with the technology; second there is the often overlooked situation of those, even in developed countries, who have had minimal exposure to the technology which is now commonplace for the majority.

Some effects of widespread use of ICT

With the widespread availability of ICT, it has been recognised that working with ICT has a significant effect on how we work and what has become more easily achievable: we can easily conduct procedures which, although not theoretically impossible in the days of paper-based records, would have been so arduous that they would not have been conducted. For example, now that major databases are accessible electronically, it is a matter of seconds to conduct a literature search spanning a number of years, using a variety of variables and, given that the researcher has the requisite skills, narrowing and widening the search easily at will. It is clear that in the days of the paper-bound version much of this research would not have taken place, either because of the long, tedious and painstaking amount of effort needed to search printed indexes or because of lack of access to such a comprehensive collection. The effect of increased research output, given online access to databases, is demonstrated by the Research4life project, which reports that research output in developing countries reveals 194 per cent increase in five years; this coincides with their being given access to online research databases (Research4life, 2009).

'Everything's on the web' we say; perhaps it is, but can everyone get access to the web? There are a number of factors militating against accessing information via the web. Of course, as in the case of developing countries, there is the issue of cost of the infrastructure and the deficit of required allied skills.

Human–computer interaction

Another important factor which may be a barrier at the individual level is web design. This has been recognised since humans first began interacting with computers. Human computer-interaction is the expanding field of research which examines how we interact with computers and, as we saw earlier, access to computers can and does change the way in which we behave. As early as 1960, the possibilities for changing how we think and work was foretold: 'In not too many years, human brains and computing machines will be coupled together very tightly, and that the resulting partnership will think as no human brain has ever thought. … To think in interaction with a computer in the same way that you think with a colleague whose competence supplements your own' (Licklider, 1960). However, to collaborate with a colleague it is necessary to be able to communicate with that colleague and this is where poor web design can frustrate the process. At the simplest level, a lack of basic familiarity with the jargon of computers and general principles of web layout can be a barrier:

> Once the user has found the online public service, they must be able to get into it and find their way round it with ease … on a point of language use, some individuals may not be familiar with even the most common computer or net terminology. In the health context for instance, usability tests revealed that for some people the 'home page' meant the part of the site that dealt with 'health in the home'. (Gunter, 2002)

Computer frustration

Frustration with interacting with computers is common. In a research report conducted at Stanford University we read of researchers' surprise at some of the findings:

> One of the most surprising findings of this research project is the time lost due to frustrating situations. In terms of minutes lost, the study subjects estimated that one-third to one-half of the time spent in front of the computer was lost, due to frustrating experiences … Much of this lost time was caused by problems with

Web navigation. This is obviously a troubling finding, pointing to the problems that users face in their everyday interactions with their computers. (Lazar and others, 2003)

Another noticeable phenomenon when inexperienced users are introduced to online databases, is that they have a tendency to credit them with *human intelligence*, so are either disconcerted when the system does not compensate for their badly phrased searches or overwhelmed by the rapidity with which the query is answered. They need to be reminded that they are in charge of the enquiry and this is only a very useful and helpful aid which will find just what it is asked, so they need to frame their queries carefully. 'Remember, it's quick, but it's thick'.

Outside the library context giving due attention to human–machine interaction is vitally important: badly designed human–machine interfaces can lead to many unexpected problems, some of devastating proportions, a classic example of this being the 'Three Mile Island' accident. Subsequent investigations concluded that the design of the human–machine interface was at least partially responsible for the disaster.

Digital divide

The second factor we should consider is that of the 'digital divide' – the updated version of the 'haves and have nots'. Given the growing role of ICT in information provision and retrieval, feeling at ease and familiar with the necessary hardware appears to be a key factor; in the Barriers to Libraries Project (Hull, 2000) one of the over-arching themes to emerge was a felt need for IT in the home, both from those who owned their own PCs and those who did not: 'And the teachers expect you to have a PC at home. ... I do think that anyone in their second or third years are so disadvantaged if they don't have their own computer. It would be awful if I didn't have ready access to IT' (male Social Sciences student, under 21). 'Some of us [overseas students] are very new to computers. It has been a struggle. I *must* get my own machine; I hope that it will improve my work' (male Engineering student, aged 31–40, from Africa).

There was evidence that the initial interaction with a computer is important in setting attitudes for later, a bad initial experience and failure to provide proper training seemingly sapping confidence for some time later. 'I first used a computer when I was temping. It was in the office and I was scared to break it. They never train you properly when you're a temporary worker. It was horrible. I'm alright *now*' (female Humanities student, aged 30–40). The need for a flexible approach to ICT training is indicated: 'As part of Learning Skills, we had 2 one hour sessions but that wasn't long enough for me and a few older people struggling a bit. The young ones were OK. I'm 44. We had extra time with X but I've still not managed to master it yet' (male Biology undergraduate, 44).

As with use of 'traditional' libraries, parental attitudes are very influential:

> I just don't like computers. They make me feel really nervous. My parents don't like them either. My father is 60 and he has had to start training to use one for his work. He had been hoping to finish his working life without having to use one, so he is really fed up ... If I get a good job and I feel I need one, I'll buy a computer for home. But I will avoid it if I possibly can. (Q 227 female, Humanities student, aged mid-20s)

Others report positive home influences in this respect: 'My Dad has always been interested in computers ... I've done a GCSE in IT and got an "A". I can do what I want in word-processing' (male student, English course, under 21).

Several years on from the Barriers to Libraries Project in the developed world, access to a computer and the Internet, although not ensuring automatic information literacy, is a condition to its achievement; ideally this would mean access to ICT in the home. In considering how far this is being achieved, NIACE's annual survey (NIACE, 2009) makes sobering reading:

One third of adults do not have regular access to computers and the Internet. Access to newer technologies tends to decline by socio-economic class:

- In 2009, 45 per cent of adults in the lowest socio-economic groups (DE) have access to a computer, compared to 70 per cent of skilled manual workers (C2s).

- Just 37 per cent of DEs have Internet access, compared to 66 per cent of C2s.

- 56 per cent of DEs have access to digital television, compared to 71 per cent of C2s.

- Only 19 per cent of DEs have digital radio, compared to 32 per cent of C2s and 44 per cent of adults in the highest socio-economic groups (AB).[1]

It is tempting to imagine the lack of contact with ICT being concentrated in households of the ageing population, those who have failed to keep up with the technology: in the 1950s there were still a few senior citizens around who were ill at ease using the telephone! But recent research reveals '3 million UK *children* still without computers or broadband ISP internet access' in the home (ISP Review, 2010). These children will have some exposure to ICT in school and in the public library but research has shown that those with a computer in the home used both the public library and college or university library more than non-computer owners: PC ownership could therefore be used as a predictor of Library use. The difference between the two categories is statistically significant for college/university library use[2] (Hull, 2000).

Information literacy

The emphasis placed on ICT literacy can lead to its conflation information literacy, which although it nowadays may rely heavily on ICT skills, is in fact much more: a person who is information literate has been defined by the American Library Association (1989) as 'able to recognize when information is needed and have the ability to locate, evaluate, and use effectively the needed information'. Webber and Johnston (2003) define it as 'the adoption of appropriate information behaviour to identify, through whatever channel or medium, information well fitted to information needs, leading to wise and ethical use of information in society'.

Notes

1. Key to classifications used: AB = professional and managerial, C1 and C2 = small employers/non-professional self-employed, lower supervisory, D = routine occupations, E = long term unemployed.
2. Chi-squared = 10.8, df = 1, p = <0.01.

References

American Library Association, Presidential Committee on Information Literacy, 24 July 2006. *www.ala.org/ala/*

mgrps/divs/acrl/publications/whitepapers/presidential.cfm (accessed 25/08/10) Document ID: 126315.

Gunter, B. (2002) 'Access does not equal success', *Update*, 1, 3, pp. 54–55.

Hull, B. (2000) 'Barriers to Libraries as agents of lifelong learning', London: Library and Information Commission, available at *http://lis.tees.ac.uk/research/researchbh.cfm* (accessed 23/09/10).

ISP Review website *www.ispreview.co.uk/story/2010/12/28/3-million-uk-children-still-without-computers-or-broadband-isp-internet-access.html* (accessed 6/01/10).

Lazar, J. and others (2003) 'Help! I'm lost: User frustration in web navigation', *IT&Society*, 1, 3, Winter 2003, pp. 18–26, *www.ITandSociety.org* (accessed 19/09/10).

Licklider, J.C.R. (1960) 'Man-computer symbiosis', *IRE Transactions on human factors in Electronics HFE1(1)* 4–11 (reprinted in Taylor, R. W. (ed.) 'In memoriam: J C R Licklider:1915–1990', Digital systems research centre Reports 61, 1990).

NIACE's Annual Survey of Digital Participation (2009), available at *www.niace.org.uk/news/over-one-in-three-adults-don%E2%80%99t-use-the-internet* (accessed 6/08/10).

Research4life (2009) 'Research output in developing countries reveals 194% increase in five years', available at *www.who.int/hinari/Increase_in_developing_country_research_output.pdf* (accessed 18/09/10).

Webber, S. and Johnston, B. (2003) 'Information literacy. Definitions and models', available *http://dis.shef.ac.uk/literacy/definitions.htm* (accessed 25/08/10).

9

Disability as a barrier

Abstract: This chapter considers some of the problems faced by the disabled, the progress made following anti-discrimination legislation and the paramount importance of staff attitudes in dealing with disabled clients.

Key words: disability, Disability Discrimination Act, staff attitudes.

Extent of disability

Disability can no longer be seen as a 'minority' problem. In the UK, out of a population of approximately 61 million, there are 10 million disabled people, of whom 5.1 million are over state pension age and 700,000 are children (Office for Disability, 2009). It is reported that 47.5 million US adults (21.8 per cent) reported a disability in 2005 (Brault, 2008).

Legislation on disability discrimination

In most developed countries there now exists legislation to prevent discrimination in accessing services because of disability. In the UK this legislation is relatively recent: the Disability Discrimination Act was passed in 1995 – the result of a long campaign. It introduced measures aimed at preventing discrimination against disabled people and gave them new rights in the areas of employment, buying and renting property and access to goods, facilities and services. It is the last of these, the access to facilities and services, which is of concern to libraries and led them to re-examine their buildings, policies and staff development issues in light of the Disability Discrimination Act. We should not imagine that these activities were starting ab initio: for example, as early as the 1980s Manchester Central Library, in the UK, owned and made available to blind readers, the relatively recently invented Kurzweil reading machine. The same library offered a separate entrance for readers in wheelchairs, who were prevented from entering via the front entrance with its flight of steps. It is interesting and possibly an influential factor that it had been a Manchester Member of Parliament, Alf Morris, who had introduced a private member's bill to Parliament which led to the passing of the 1970 Chronically Sick & Disabled Persons Act, a ground-breaking step on the road to equality; this legislation was the first in the world to recognise and give rights to people with disabilities. The Act has been described as 'a Magna Carta for the disabled' – at the time, it was revolutionary in transforming official policy (BBC, 2010). No doubt many other examples exist of caring, pre-Disability Discrimination Act attempts to provide disabled patrons with a level playing field.

In common with many other public buildings, libraries have become far more accessible to wheelchair users in recent years and this is to be applauded. Larger libraries frequently have reading machines and other adaptive technology which has opened previously locked doors. But disability is not always obvious: two commonly overlooked disabilities are partial hearing loss and failing eyesight, on the increase as the population of the developed world ages. While not as obvious as being totally deaf or blind, in practical terms it is almost as debilitating, although not recognised and catered for.

Libraries in the UK have embraced the demands of the Disability Discrimination Act, understandably, with varying degrees of enthusiasm. Some older buildings, without lifts, do not lend themselves easily to disabled access: I do remember in the early 1990s working in a college where the library was on the first floor with no lift. Theoretically, disabled students could access by a chairlift, which was frequently out of order. In practice, one disabled student, a mere slip of a girl, was frequently carried up and down the staircase by a strong porter. 'Where there's a will' – yes indeed, but can we imagine the embarrassment for that student and possibly for a notional one who weighed 250+pounds?

All staff to be disability-aware

In the UK, SCONUL (Society of College national and University Libraries) has produced a very comprehensive guide to access for disabled library users (Robertson, 2007).

Gillian Burrington, a British information professional who became blind later in life, is in a unique position to give us an informed insight into the serious limitations in a blind person fully satisfying his/her information needs. Some of these problems can arise because of a lack of staff awareness at the operational level. She writes:

> I was heavily involved with the Library Association (now the Chartered Institute of Library and Information Professionals [CILIP]) from 1987 to 1998 and was its president in 1994. The Library Association was

committed to equal opportunities, and all my papers were automatically sent to me in large print or on disk. Some years later I asked to receive the journal of our new institution in an accessible format. To my surprise I was told that this would not be possible. I made several suggestions as to how it could be done but these were all rejected by staff at the operational level. Only when I took the issue to the chief executive was it made plain that CILIP's policy, the culture of the organization, and the spirit of the DDA meant that my needs had to be met. This clearly demonstrates that any equal opportunities policy is useless unless everyone in the organization is made aware of it. Equally important, people need to know what it is possible to do as well as knowing the organization's legal responsibilities. I believe this applies as much to libraries as to any other professional association. (Burrington, 2007)

When as an information professional in the 1990s, tasked with provision of university library services to the disabled, I held forums with disabled readers, there was a recurring theme when they articulated their needs and expectations of the library service: the *attitudes* of staff are as important, if not more important, than provision of all the latest gadgetry.

The importance of staff attitudes is highlighted by McCaskill and Goulding (2001) in an article investigating public library compliance with the Disability Discrimination Act 1995:

Key importance of attitudes

Attitudinal discrimination refers to the way that individuals view or treat those with disabilities. In public libraries there is considerable scope for attitudinal discrimination which might include making assumptions about disabled people's library needs, for example, or what they can and cannot cope with in the library. Attitudinal discrimination can also include staff patronising disabled library users or being impatient or discourteous. A lack of general disability awareness among library staff can also be a large attitudinal barrier.

Additionally, Charles (2005) in an article on disability awareness training in libraries concludes:

> While library managers and planners have to work out what major changes have to be made to conform with the Disability Discrimination Act, those of us who meet our readers with disabilities can do a lot to improve the quality of service they receive simply by doing some basic disability awareness training and remembering the key points which will help to provide them with the sort of service we aim to provide for everyone. However, the most important message to take out of disability awareness training remains: person first, disability second.

The classic mistake, made by the 'normal' part of the population, of assuming that because someone has a disability in one area that they are totally incompetent in every other way possible is often dubbed the 'Does he take sugar?' syndrome. We all feel justifiably incensed if discussions about our needs and desires are made in our presence without our opinion being sought. Children are irritated by adults who speak about them as if they were not there; imagine how grown adults feel.

'Does he take sugar in his tea?'
Hello; why not ask me?
I might have a disability,
But to answer for myself I still have the ability. (Williams, 2011)

The uninitiated often feel inadequate in the face of a disability of which they have no knowledge and the 'Does he take sugar?' is a classic overreaction. The general rule of thumb for helping a disabled person is to *ask* them *if* help is needed and if so, *what* kind of help. From my discussions with disabled clients, I know that they do not want to be pitied or patronised; what they do value is low key matter-of-fact assistance to help them access resources open to the majority.

An interesting example of how the library can be of real practical help to some disabled students, in the very widest sense, facilitating their integration into the mainstream, is described by Susan Jaworski of Buffalo State College, where staff members at E. H. Butler Library, Buffalo State College, have collaborated with programmes to help make inclusivity and diversity more than just buzzwords (Jaworski, 2009). The scheme allows students, young people aged 18–23 who have completed high school and have a wide range of developmental disabilities, to participate in an inclusive, age-appropriate learning environment, acquiring job skills as well as social skills that will prepare them for the workplace. The scheme warrants mention because it demonstrates a breadth of spirit that recognises that the definition of 'normal' is quite arbitrary. Although the use of volunteers in libraries is far from unique, this one recognises the values of attributes viewed as abnormal, 'character traits once thought to be symptoms of a disability now turned out to be job skills. Autism, a disorder that expounds repetitive behavior, can find an ally in shelving books, shelf reading and filing'

(Jaworski, 2009). By being given responsibilities and the opportunity to do a 'normal' job, these volunteers develop the social skills that come from interacting with others and a number have gone on to obtain 'real' paid employment.

Thanks to the huge advances in enabling technology, and in contrast to past decades, the disabled continue to participate more fully in mainstream society. We must match the technological progress with a progressive enlightenment of our attitudes.

References

Brault, M. (2008) 'Americans with disabilities: 2005', current population reports, P70–117, Washington, DC: US Census Bureau.

BBC (2010) 'Four decades since Alf Morris' landmark disability act', available at *http://news.bbc.co.uk/local/ manchester/hi/people_and_places/newsid_8697000/ 8697567.stm* (accessed 22/10/10).

Burrington, G.A. (2007) 'A user's perspective', *Library Trends*, Vol. 55, No. 4, Spring 2007 ('Library and Information Services for Visually Impaired People', edited by Helen Brazier and David Owen), pp. 760–766.

Charles, S. (2005) 'Person first, disability second: disability awareness training in libraries', *Library Review*, 54(8), pp. 453–458.

Jaworski, S. (2009) 'How a library can develop the ability in disability', Paper presented at 2009 NYLA Annual Conference & Trade Show, Niagara Falls, New York, NYLA Diversity Fair, 15 October 2009.

McCaskill, K. and Goulding, A. (2001) 'English public library services and the Disability Discrimination Act', *New Library World*, 102(1165), pp. 192–206.

Office for Disability (2009) 'Disability prevalence estimates', available at *www.officefordisability.gov.uk/docs/res/fact sheets/disability-prevalence* (accessed 22/10/10).

Robertson, L. on behalf of the SCONUL Access Steering Group (2007) 'Access for library users with disabilities', Society of College National and University Libraries, available at *www.sconul.ac.uk/publications/pubs/access_disabilities.pdf* (accessed 15/10/10).

Williams, M.W. (2011) 'Poems from from Connah's Quay', available at *www.bbc.co.uk/wales/northeast/sites/poetry/pages/michael_williams.shtml* (accessed 5/01/11).

10

Clarity of purpose

Abstract: This chapter emphasises the need for the library to have a clarity of purpose that is conveyed to staff at all levels. It examines the value of mission statements and slogans and the need for these to be translated into strategic goals and operational guidelines and the need for all staff to follow library policy.

Key words: mission statements, strategic goals, operational guidelines, adherence to policy.

What are you trying to achieve here?

At the risk of sounding rather facetious, does the management of your library and, perhaps as importantly, the rank and file, really have a *crystal clear* idea of what the library is trying to achieve? Sometimes it can be very illuminating to speak to some of the more seasoned junior library staff, 'off the record', and see how their interpretation of the library's purpose matches up to the official one: sometimes the deviation is because they have not been kept up to speed by staff development so do not feel they are stakeholders in the organisation. At other times it may be because they personally disagree with the 'new-fangled' ways of doing things. As we saw in the chapter entitled 'What are libraries for?', particularly in the case of public libraries, there has been considerable change in the way they are being projected to potential users. Some older people, both library employees and patrons, think back wistfully to the days when visiting the library was more like entering a cathedral than a coffee bar. Folk memories do not change overnight ...

The client group

Most libraries service the needs of a particular client group or community and consequently should be run in the best way to achieve that goal; ideally, this will involve liaison with the users of the service, to help to identify more accurately the needs of the client group. Although this is a partnership venture, one of the library's roles in this relationship should be an advisory, educative one: it is reasonable to expect information professionals to be more fully appraised than their client groups on the availability of relevant sources of information and the best ways of accessing them. After all, that is what we *do*! Our users have their own, different, lives to lead and, while they may be keen and loyal supporters of the library, it is rarely at the top of their list of priorities and they are not as aware of the minutiae of stock and services as those employed in the library service. Unfortunately, the less thoughtful believe that they do know it all already. In the British Library-funded Barriers to Libraries Project (Hull, 2000), for example, it was found that 'there seems to be a mismatch between the sample's perception of their information retrieval skills and the actual barriers they encounter ... These attitudes must represent the greatest barriers of all – not only do they not know, they are not *aware* that they do not know.' So part of the library's remit should be to educate on what it can/could do. A library service, while taking account of the wishes of its client group, should not be a mere knee jerk reaction to what the client group perceives as its needs; the service should also be informed by the library staff's knowledge, expertise and experience; part of a library's remit is to *educate*. As Henry Ford is famously reported as saying, 'If I'd have asked my customers what they wanted, they'd have said a faster horse.'

Another, extremely important, factor shaping the delivery of the service is budgetary controls: not many libraries are self-sufficient, having to rely on external funding, either from the parent institution or a government body. When those holding the purse strings are not well-informed on library matters, there is the danger of inappropriate restrictions caused by their lack of vision. Time and effort spent on clear communication with funders is well spent. The liaison role with those in budgetary control is a delicate one but the library will gain little by failing to state its needs clearly and assertively, thereby making it less likely to be seen as a soft target for any future cuts.

Mission statements

A way of stating the library's purpose is through its mission statement, an expression originally associated with mission-aries propagating the gospel and adopted by the business world. A mission statement has been defined as:

> a formal, short, written statement of the purpose of a *company* or *organization*. The mission statement should guide the actions of the organization, spell out its overall goal, provide a sense of direction, and guide decision-making. It provides the framework or context

within which the company's strategies are formulated. (Mission statements, 2010)

A very clear straightforward guide to mission statement writing is available from the Chartered Institute of Marketing (2009).

Mission statements have been the source of much debate and a good deal of denigration:

> Mission statements have a bad reputation. Many people think of them as mere words on paper, with messages so general and sappy that they are meaningless and could apply to any firm, so obvious that they hardly need mentioning, or full of lies and political correctness, purporting that the organization values things that employees and customers know it does not, with the end results that no-one will pay any attention to them anyway. (Kross, 2002)

I disagree: one of the purposes of mission statements is to offer to staff a *desirable ideal*; if you aim high, you get higher than if you aim low! Peter Drucker, the celebrated business guru, recognised that it is more important that firms know what the 'business should be' than what '[the] business is'. Drucker (1974) and Morphew and Hartley (2006), after conducting an analysis of mission statements from a variety of educational institutions, found that:

> our thinking may need to be updated. Simple assumptions about mission statements (e.g., they are meaningless, self-aggrandizing documents; they are essential to the planning process, etc.) may need to be rethought. While there is evidence that mission statements are used to signal and symbolize, it seems more likely

that the subject of college and university mission statements is more complex and that institutions are using these documents to communicate their utility and willingness to serve in terms that are both normative and politically apt.

One problem with many mission statements is that they tend to be rather wordy. A colleague advises me that at a recent leadership training course, although the participants were aware that their institution *had* a mission statement, only a small percentage could actually summon it to mind, which bodes ill for the rest of the staff remembering it: it might also be helpful for an organisation to adopt a much briefer, succinct statement, rather like a logo or motto, that staff can easily remember and associate with. The motto of the Royal Air Force springs to mind: 'Per ardua ad astra',[1] which has evidently served well to spur airmen on to great things – although it is not suggested that currently conceived mottos be in Latin.

Apart from serving to inspire the workforce, mission statements have other roles, serving generally to inform other stakeholders, such as the community served and those providing their finances. At the very least, as a clear statement of intent, they serve as a focus for debate or complaint if any of the stakeholders believe that the organisation is not honouring its stated mission. Adherence to a culture of transparency has been widely accepted as a desirable goal in many fields; e.g., 'In recent years, many governments have worked to increase openness and transparency in their actions' (Bertot, Jaeger and Grimes, 2010), and 'Nurse managers played a key role in creating a culture of transparency and in being a resource for error disclosures' (Shannon and others, 2009). This culture is also applicable to libraries.

The use of the mission statement has been adopted widely by the business sector where success is defined in monetary terms. The following statement, formulated after the conduct of a research project, may be seen as apposite in terms of the utility of constructing an effective mission statement: 'Mission statements that include phrases that refer to what many may view as the fundamental rules of business have a significant positive relationship with financial performance: be concerned with your employees, be responsible to the society in which you do business, and emphasize and communicate your value system' (Bartkus, Glassman and McAfee, 2006). Profitability, referred to here as 'financial performance', does not nullify the use of this advice in constructing a library mission statement. 'There is tendency to assume "profitably" equates only to money. It is possible to profit in a non-financial way' (CILIP, 2009).

For the benefit of both management and rank and file, it is clear that the idealistic aims of the mission statement need to be translated into more manageable objectives or 'service strategic goals'. While the overall mission statement may remain the same, the service strategic goals are likely to change from year to year. Unlike the mission statement, which some members of staff may be unable to produce verbatim, every member of staff, at whatever level in the hierarchy, should be well acquainted with the library's strategic goals, that of their team or section and preferably their own personal ones. It is advisable for staff to be reminded of current strategic goals at regular intervals, either by means of intranets, e-mails or preferably staff meetings. This will communicate to everyone the importance of the library's goals, that these are not just the responsibility of senior management and that everybody's contribution to the overall achievement of these goals is recognised and valued.

Operational guidelines

There is also a very real need for clear cut operational guidelines for junior staff to follow, from which there should be no deviation without reference to the highest level. Nothing is more irritating to a library user than knowing that the facilities available to them depend on the whim or prejudice of the staff member with whom they are interacting. Young male students, for example, have been overheard saying: 'The one with the long hair doesn't charge you fines, if you flirt with her a bit', which is not very helpful to female students or middle aged male ones.

As is suggested in the chapter on staff development, all staff should be encouraged to contribute to the debate on library policy and practice. Their suggestions should be considered when formulating policy, but this is not the same as operating in the situation where policy is improvised on the hoof. Working without agreed and observed operational guidelines can only lead to anarchy: a classic example of the chaos caused by a lack of clear guidelines is the variety of reasons given by some public library counter staff for deciding, on their own initiative, to waive fines: 'She looked hard up. I felt sorry for her', 'He's an old man, reminds me of my Dad', and my favourites; being, 'I didn't think nuns had to pay fines. They don't have any money, do they?' The amount of the fines waived is of no real consequence; what might be is the feelings of another reader, equally hard up but who did not look it, who did have to pay fines! It is also not conducive to job satisfaction for the staff if a clear idea of what is expected of them has not been communicated.

A final thought as we live in a culture of evaluation – we need a clear idea of what we are trying to achieve, if we are even going to approach any meaningful evaluation of it.

Note

1. 'Through adversity to the stars'.

References

Bartkus, B., Glassman, M. and McAfee, B. (2006) 'Mission Statement Quality and Financial Performance', *European Management Journal*, 24, 1, pp. 86–94.

Bertot, J.C., Jaeger, P.T. and Grimes, J.M. (2010) 'Using ICTs to create a culture of transparency: E-government and social media as openness and anti-corruption tools for societies', *Government Information Quarterly*, 27, 3, pp. 264–71.

Chartered Institute of Marketing (2009) 'Ten minute guide. Mission statements', available at *www.cim.co.uk/resources/plansandstrategy/home.aspx* (accessed 14/01/11).

CILIP (2009) 'Practical Guide: Marketing Your Library & Information Service (Part 1)', available at *www.cilip.org.uk/membership/benefits/informed/practical-guides/pages/marketing.aspx*.

Drucker, P.F. (1974) *Management: Tasks, Responsibilities, Practices*, New York: Harper & Row.

Kross, A. (2002) 'Mission statements: effective tools for change', in Kelly, M.C. and Kross, A. (eds), *Making the Grade: Academic Libraries and Student Success*, Chicago: American Library Association.

Mission statements (2010), Wikipedia *http://en.wikipedia.org/wiki/Mission_statement* (accessed 28/10/10).

Morphew, P.C. and Hartley, M. (2006) 'Mission statements: a thematic analysis of rhetoric across institutional type'. *Journal of Higher Education*, 77, 3, pp. 456–71.

Shannon, S.E. and others (2009) 'Disclosing errors to patients: Perspectives of registered nurses', *Joint Commission Journal on Quality and Patient Safety*, 35, pp. 5–12.

11

Evaluation and the value of systematic research

Abstract: This chapter considers the growth of evidence based practice and considers the caution needed in using any data, either quantitative or qualitative. The value of disseminating the results of formal research is recognised, with a plea for this to be presented in a number of formats.

Key words: research methods, qualitative data, quantitative data, formal research, surveys, evidence based practice.

Culture of evaluation

The evaluation culture in libraries is largely a product of the late 20th century, although there is earlier evidence of the wish to ascertain how well the library is performing in terms of user satisfaction – an interesting overview of which is provided by Crawford (2006). Since the turn of the century there has been a general growing emphasis on evidence based practice, particularly in the field of medicine. As early as 1997, Eldredge was calling for evidence based librarianship and published a seminal article 'Evidence-based librarianship: an overview' in 2000 (Eldredge, 2000). The principle has been further debated and adopted by some in the library profession, with a number of acronyms emerging to represent the activity. One such is Evidence-Based Library and Information Practice (EBLIP) which seeks to improve library and information services and practice by bringing together the best available evidence and insights derived from working experience, moderated by user needs and preferences. EBLIP involves asking answerable questions, finding, critically appraising and then utilising research evidence from relevant disciplines in daily practice. It thus attempts to integrate user-reported, practitioner-observed and research-derived evidence as an explicit basis for decision-making. (Booth, 2006)

For many practitioners the prospect of practising EBLIP may seem daunting, although a Toolkit is freely available online. The key issue in evaluating is the formation of the questions of what should be evaluated. 'Questions drive the entire EBL process. EBL assigns highest priority to posed questions with greatest relevance to library practice. The wording & content of the questions will determine what kinds of research designs are needed to secure answers' (Eldredge, 2000).

What are we measuring?

At a more mundane level, it would be a rare library today which was not obliged by the funder or parent organisation to keep a record of what are often termed 'performance measurements' or 'performance indicators'. Unfortunately, if insufficient thought is given to the process, this can lead to the measurement of that which is easily measurable, such as heating and printing costs or the mentality of crude 'cost effectiveness' applied, say, to the number of times a particular book title has been issued. If, for example, a book on women's assertiveness is potentially of great personal benefit to women in the particular community served by the library, that potential benefit to individuals is in no way diminished if it is borrowed only eight or nine times, rather than the round figure of ten arbitrarily plucked from the ether by someone in the finance department, as representative of 'value for money'. If Library A provides coffee bar facilities and clerical support at a smaller unit cost than Library B, is it a 'better' library? The promotion of these formulaic principles is alien to the philosophical aims of information provision, with its potential for encouraging the wider personal growth of the individual. An approach which advocates measuring success only by what is easily measurable, springs from an ignorance of these philosophical aims. Besides, library staff at grass roots level sometimes find ways of 'massaging' statistics which they know do not accurately represent the true value of what is happening; it is almost a tradition for mobile libraries visiting far-flung rural communities to persuade users to take the maximum number of books allowed, rather than the one or two they have carefully chosen, warning that the service might well suffer if the issue statistics are not healthy. This is a good reminder for us that 'books issued' does not equal 'books read'.

Treat statistics with caution

Manipulating statistics to achieve a goal occurs elsewhere: interesting tactics have been employed by students in Adult Education classes, say where a minimum class size of 15 has been prescribed in the name of viability. If perhaps only 14 have enrolled, it is not unknown for these 14 to club together to pay the enrolment fee for a 15th person and a compliant friend who is not interested in the subject of the class, who just appears at the first class to get a name on the register, then disappears, never to be seen again. So statistics can be made to give an untrue picture. Other interesting examples of the misuse of statistics may be found at the website 'How To Understand Statistics' (BBC). This is not to dismiss completely the use of statistics, but just to remind us that they can be used to lie – 'Lies, damned lies and statistics'.[1]

While quantitative data, assuming that it has been accurately collected, can provide a partial picture of what is happening, it does no more than that. The impression we form from considering opening hours statistics does, on the one hand, tell the extent of physical access made possible for client groups but on the other it does not tell us how much real benefit they are drawing from being there. During the 1930s Depression in the UK, library folklore tells us that many visitors to the public library were motivated more by the desire to keep warm and dry, than the wish to read. The traditional yardstick used to assess the true motive was whether the reader succeeded in remaining awake, with anyone actually falling asleep and snoring being asked to leave. More recently, with some universities introducing 24/7 access, those with inner urban sites reported similar problems of some 'inappropriate' use in the hours normally devoted to sleep. So in this case, counting the number of patrons through the door only provides us with a *partial* picture.

To capture more fully what is happening we would also need access to qualitative data, which is notoriously difficult to capture. For example, to attempt to ascertain perfectly the significance of the library service to its users would involve an enormous amount of data collection. Besides collecting the minutiae of the statistical data on each individual, such as time spent using online subscription databases, number of books borrowed, etc., it would also involve collecting qualitative data, probably gained through interview, of the user's perceptions of the service. Even if such an exercise were feasible, it would still not provide a perfect picture because even in an unstructured interview, where the respondent is not confined to answering closed questions, some individuals, for a variety of reasons, do not give completely frank and truthful responses in interviews. They may be afraid of demonstrating their ignorance or they may want to please the interviewer by giving the 'right' answer.

Therefore, in view of the fact that any data, however carefully it has been collected and whether it is quantitative or qualitative, should be treated with caution – we can never really know the truth; we only have access to a versions of the truth. The most important potential benefits of libraries, in the wider philosophical term, are notoriously difficult to capture and quantify and an individual library is unlikely to have the staff time or expertise available for an ambitious project of this nature, which may more properly be the subject of centrally funded or partnership initiatives. Gorman (2009) indicates that the quest for the truth continues:

> However, to a great degree we lack measures that fall between the Scylla of bean counting and the Charybdis of subjective measures of perception. It is incumbent on us, therefore, to develop new nuanced measures that address the value of the library to the university— measures that deal with real educational and societal outcomes and that demonstrate to all that which we know in our hearts—that a truly educated person is one who can interact autonomously with the human record with confidence and skill.

Difficulties in collecting good quality data

McNicol (2003), in a survey of UK academic libraries, found that although many academic librarians expressed an interest in conducting research projects 'the main constraints on institutions becoming involved in further research were lack of time and lack of finances with fifty out of sixty-two respondents (81 per cent) citing lack of time as an issue and forty-one (66 per cent) claiming lack of finances were a barrier to research'. Of course this does not preclude non-researchers from benefitting from the research findings of others and it is incumbent on those conducting research projects to report their findings in a variety of styles, of which some should be in easily digestible format. Some extremely capable practitioner librarians are discouraged from reading research reports because of their opacity: not everyone is familiar with 't tests' and 'chi squared' and better communication with *more* of our peers is facilitated if there are various versions of research findings available. The more accessible the research findings are, the wider will be their readership and the greater will be the likelihood of them being discussed and informing the improvement of libraries. Making a personal observation I would say that, before I had had a thorough grounding in advanced research methods, I was certainly discouraged from reading arcane accounts of research projects.

But even if we cannot all undertake large time-consuming formal research, we can gain valuable insights both by our own reflections, as detailed more fully in Chapter 12 'Reflective practice', and by communicating with our users.

Besides the daily feedback, accessible to anyone who takes the time to listen and which would provide substance for their reflection, there are other, more formal, means of communicating with users: library committees, user panels, focus groups, feedback forms, suggestion boxes and surveys. These ideas are not new, but they can work to improve communications. I have found, for example, that attending course boards, where there was a standing item, 'Library issues' was an extremely rich source of contact with users and an excellent way of strengthening and clarifying communication with both staff and students.

Surveys

One way of trying to access the library's users to ascertain their evaluation and desires is via a library survey. Hiller (2001) sounds a word of caution for any library considering a survey:

> Whether the survey questions are statistically reliable, representative, valid or significant doesn't necessarily mean that they provide information that can be used to assess and improve library service quality. It is also important to examine whether these surveys are asking the right questions in the right way to the right group. Survey design is a complex and evolving process that requires substantial interaction between the surveying group and the surveyed population.

Because of the sheer complexity of the process of constructing the survey instrument, it may be advisable to use survey instruments compiled by experts, possibly by the group to which the library belongs, e.g. SCONUL. Creaser (2006) provides an excellent comparison and analysis of two survey instruments used in UK academic libraries: the LibQual+ surveys as they have been applied in the UK, and the standard SCONUL user survey template. We are reminded that:

> One aim of user surveys must be to improve the services provided to users. High overall satisfaction levels are good for publicity, and may persuade institutional management that all is well with the library, but they should not lead to complacency within the service. It is important to drill down into the detail of the results, to make comparisons within or between services, and to investigate examples of good practice. (Creaser, 2006)

It is commendable that in the information profession there is continuing healthy debate on how well we are performing and how best this may be captured.

Note

1. Mark Twain.

References

Booth, A. (2006) 'Counting what counts: performance measurement and evidence-based practice', *Performance Measurement and Metrics*, 7 (2), pp. 63–74.

BBC (2011) 'How To Understand Statistics', *www.bbc.co.uk/dna/h2g2/A1091350* (accessed 26/01/11).

Crawford, J. (2006) *The culture of evaluation in library and information services*, Oxford: Chandos Publishing.

Creaser, C. (2006) 'One size does not fit all: user surveys in academic libraries', *Performance Measurement and Metrics*, 7, 3, pp. 153–62.

EBLIP Toolkit (2010) Available at *www.newcastle.edu.au/ service/library/gosford/ebl/toolkit/* (accessed 2/12/10).

Eldredge, J.D. (1997) 'Evidence based librarianship: a commentary for Hypothesis', *Hypothesis*, 11(3), pp. 4–7.

Eldredge, J.D. (2000) 'Evidence based librarianship: an overview', *Bull Med Libr Assoc*, 88(4) October 2000.

Gorman, M. (2009) 'The louder they talked of outcomes, the faster we counted our beans. Measuring the impact of academic libraries', SCONUL, London, 29 November 2009.

Hiller, S. (2001) 'Assessing user needs, satisfaction and library performance at the University of Washington Libraries', *Library Trends* 49, 4, pp. 605–25.

McNicol, S. (2003) 'Research in academic libraries: a survey of practitioners', SCONUL Newsletter 29 Summer/ Autumn 2003.

12

Librarians as reflective practitioners

Abstract: This chapter gives a brief overview of reflective practice in general terms and its potential practical relevance for the information professional. Some examples are given of changes made as the result of applying the principles of reflective practice. The changes resulting from reflective practice, while being informative in other situations, are not necessarily transferable in their original form.

Key words: reflective practice, information professionals, librarians, changes to services.

What is meant by reflective in this context? The *Oxford English Dictionary* (2004) defines reflection as 'the action of turning (back) or fixing the thoughts on some subject; meditation, deep or serious consideration'.

General growth of reflective practice

'The Reflective Practitioner' (Schön, 1983) popularised the term reflective practice although the concepts supporting it go back even further: John Dewey had already written about reflective practice, and other researchers such Jean Piaget, William James and Carl Jung had investigated the theories of human learning. Central to the development of reflective theory was interest in how human beings integrate theory and practice, the cyclical pattern of our experience and how we consciously apply that learning experience. Over the past 30 years, there has been an increased focus on experiential learning and the development and application of reflective practice. Schön's book introduces concepts such as 'reflection on action' and 'reflection in-action' where professionals meet the challenges of their work by improvising what they have learned in practice. An example of 'reflection *in* action' might occur during a training session when you become aware, and act upon, the need to rearrange the layout of the room so that all participants can watch a demonstration. An example of 'reflection *on* action' might occur after a team meeting, when you consider how you responded to a particular comment or criticism, how this made you feel, what you have learnt from that experience, and how you might respond in the future.

The concept of reflective practice is now accepted and used by organisations, networks, and individuals. It has been adopted widely by the medical profession. An experienced nursing sister told me that the way she, as a young cadet at Nursing School, had been taught to prepare the dressings trolley was so time-consuming and unnecessarily complicated that the first time she had carefully followed the procedure on the ward, she had been gently ridiculed by experienced colleagues. They had clearly seen the possibility for stream-lining procedures by eliminating the unnecessary and saving precious time for more useful activities. In the nursing profession, like many others, there used to be a gulf between theory as taught and practice as practised but in recent years the concept of the reflective practitioner has been widely adopted.

As professionals, it is desirable for us to take some time to reflect on what we are doing and how well it is achieving our desired goals, rather than fall into the trap of believing that if something has always been done in a particular way, or because some 'expert' prescribes it, that it must be right; for example, in the 1960s there was a surge in the publication of baby care books, in place of relying on the folk wisdom transmitted via the family. Of course much of the advice was theoretical with no grounding in reality and no acknowledgement of the fact that every human being is unique and all babies are not the same! Stressed out new mothers were not infrequently heard to observe that, although *they* had read lots of advice, unfortunately, 'The baby hasn't read the book' and so did not behave as predicted.

We can and do learn from reading books by 'experts' in our field of endeavour and this gives us a sound foundation on which to build. But the practitioner in the field is confronted with the reality, not the theory. The mantra of tutors in colleges of education, when students sought advice on how to deal with discipline problems in the classroom, used to be 'If your lessons are interesting, you won't have any discipline problems'. It was noticeable that a fair proportion of students dropped out of the course after the first teaching practice. Children with problems at home bring their angst to school and, no matter how interesting the lesson may be, will be disruptive, given the opportunity. Experienced teachers in the school are usually willing to share their tricks of the trade, but they rarely serve as more than a starting point. Only by reflecting on one's own performance can a modus operandi, appropriate to this particular situation, be found.

In the same vein, we might learn the classic ideal on our library and information courses, and share experiences with our colleagues working in similar areas and activities to be commended. But very few of these can be assimilated in their raw form – they will be more effective if they are adapted to our own situation. A frequent, but nonetheless valid, observation is that every situation is unique. We should respect and value our own perceptions, to which we can gain access through quiet reflection.

Failure to consider change, and complacency, should be anathema to a caring professional. Following the posting of a query on a general library discussion list on how libraries deal with non-standard users, such as non-native speakers or those with disabilities, a rather, to me, depressing reply was received from a college library: that all their users were treated as 'standard users' in tours and seminars, although care was taken to speak slowly if non-native speakers of English had been identified, and anyone with a disability was asked to say whether they needed any extra help. Finally, the respondent went on to express the belief that the library services were appreciated but no specific feedback was sought from disabled users so that they would not feel they were being treated differently from anyone else. No doubt this individual and organisation are well intentioned and caring in their own estimation, but they could possibly change their approach if they reflected on their actions: first, how many non-native speakers, who have made the mistake of not looking 'foreign', have slipped through the net? Second, how many not *obviously* disabled people have not received the help they need? Third, how do they know how they could improve, if users are never given the chance to give feedback or suggestions? To consider the first two points above, if the library has good communication links with other departments they should *know* in advance if an induction group has non-native speakers or disabled students in it and act accordingly. The final comment seems to be indicative of self satisfaction and complacency.

A professional's act of reflection can encompass all that they do and has two aspects: first the continuous kind of reflection that should be an ongoing part of our daily professional life (Schön's reflection in action); second, the more substantial act of reflection, which may take several days, that we need to make periodically, say annually, when we review the past year in the light of our stated values and goals and plan for the forthcoming year (Schön's reflection on action).

A personal reflective 'log'

It is worthwhile, for a reflective practitioner, to keep a simple daily log of one's reflections. When this log is perused at intervals, over a period, new ideas often emerge spontaneously from this data, suggestive of changes: ideas for possible new activities, possible new interpretations of old activities. This idea is loosely based on the principles of grounded theory advanced by Glaser and Strauss (1968) where theory is generated from the data.

Some reflections can lead to almost immediate changes in practice, especially if no costs are involved; e.g., if a chair for the enquirer at the Information desk has, till you arrived, always been placed to face the librarian, suggestive of confrontation, it is a simple and cost-free change to move it to the side of the desk, which subconsciously implies collaboration between librarian and enquirer. Most people have read or at least heard about the power of body language but do not always think of applying some of the ideas.

Practical outcomes from log-keeping

Some of the day to day reflections would imply more ambitious changes, which cannot be implemented straight away if they involve costs or impinge on the work of others, but it is sensible to log them in readiness for the year end reflective process. Other staff should be encouraged to reflect on what they are doing and how they are doing it, to log their reflections and to discuss their thoughts with colleagues. Opportunities for this should be part of the library organisation. Meetings have a bad press, having the reputation for wasting time talking about it, instead of doing it. If this is true, blame may be laid at the door of the chair, who should keep the meeting on track! An interesting result of reflection in-action came to a member of a group, scheduled to meet weekly, where the appointed *chairman* was ineffective and inefficient, which meant that the meetings were often tedious and overly long and therefore non-productive. It was suggested that the more junior members of the group would gain valuable professional experience from taking turns at being the chair. Because those members of staff taking turns at being the 'rotating chair' (yes, lots of jokes) were keen to do the job well, the meetings became much more focused and useful.

There are many instances of improvements that have been made following reflection of the library's and institution's aims. Here are two examples of good practice which arose from reflecting on the requirements of the Disability Discrimination Act, the institutional policy to provide disabled users with as level a playing field as possible and at the same time to have regard for any user's self-perceived 'loss of face'.

When leading tours of a new heavily-used library, where the agreed policy was for lifts to be available only to those with a disability, tour groups are always asked if anyone would like to use the lift. Seeing the notice, 'Disabled only', next to the lift a member of one group quipped, 'Do we *look* disabled?' and was surprised by the reply 'No, you don't, but lots of disabilities are not obvious'. I have a friend with a cardiac condition who wishes others had reflected a little before suggesting everyone climbs three flights of stairs, 'because it'll be quicker'.

In a university library which has excellent liaison links with its disabilities officer, recognising that all disabilities are not obvious, it was agreed that it would be impossible for all library staff to identify all disabled patrons and a discreet form of identification was needed, possibly using the students' library membership cards. Acknowledging that nobody wants to be 'labelled', the addition of the word 'disabled' was rejected, even the letter D was thought to be too obvious. After reflection, it was decided that, on library registration, an extra broad blue stripe be incorporated onto the disabled users' cards, a message only recognisable to the initiated. The system worked very well and the significance of the blue stripe was incorporated into all staff induction training.

Since the turn of the century, there has been more interest shown in reflective practice in Library and Information circles; Grant (2007), for example, published a systematic review of the specific area and concluded:

> The dispersed nature of the reflective accounts identified in this review are both a cause of celebration and concern. A celebration because it demonstrates the global interest within the library and information sector in using reflection as a means of continued professional development. The broad publication base also expands the chances of those new to the concept of reflection encountering it and evaluating its potential contribution to their own development. However, the dispersed nature of publications could make it difficult for others to identify examples of good practice from which to learn.

In a review of this work by Grant, Perryman (2008) points out that it does not satisfy all the criteria required for a classic systematic review and that 'The study might have been better approached as an initial review of the literature, as a way to assess the status of reflection in (or on) practice.'

In my opinion, both these writers seem to have missed the essential *spirit* of reflective practice. It is a personal activity in/on a particular situation which leads to improvements in that situation even though any improvements it stimulates may be useful for consideration in other situations. It would be regrettable if information workers were to be discouraged from using reflective practice because they felt they were not performing the process along strict guidelines, using the approved jargon to describe their activity. Many of the changes to practice it generates (reflection in practice) may be relatively small and cheap to implement, but significant in terms of service provision.

As the two authors above have stated, reflective practice, no doubt, has not always been referred to as 'reflective practice' by thinking librarians planning their service provision. Given that reflective practice has already been widely adopted in other highly respectable professions, it would seem preferable initially to encourage its wider adoption by those working in information rather than being overly concerned with too closely documenting the activity; that should follow naturally.

References

Glaser, B.G. and Strauss, A.L. (1968) *The Discovery of Grounded Theory: Strategies for Qualitative Research*, London: Weidenfield and Nicolson.

Grant, M.J. (2007) 'The Role of Reflection in the Library and Information Sector: A Systematic Review', *Health Information and Libraries Journal*, 24, 3, pp. 155–66.

Oxford English Dictionary (2004) Oxford: Oxford University Press.

Perryman, C. (2008) 'Further Study is Needed to Define and Measure the Use of Reflective Practice in Library and Information Science', *Evidence Based Library and Information Practice*, 2008, 3, 1, pp. 53–6.

Schön, D. (1983) *The Reflective Practitioner: How Professionals Think in Action*, New York: Basic Books.

13

Staff development

Abstract: This chapter examines staff development, considers different kinds of staff motivation, and respecting staff as individuals. It also looks at the staff development needed for volunteers and student employees.

Key words: staff development, staff motivation, respect for staff, volunteers, student employees.

Differences in motivation

It is hard to resist succumbing to the cliché 'Staff are our greatest asset', because of its essential underlying truth. However, to be worthy of this epithet, staff need to be motivated and not everyone is motivated in the same way. Some, the self-starters, are *intrinsically* motivated: they want to do a job well because they recognise that it is something worth doing and will be of benefit either to themselves or others. Those who are *extrinsically* motivated may be very hard-working and efficient but are driven by the rewards associated with the job; this could be monetary rewards or abstractions such as praise or enhanced reputation. Most people have a mixture of both kinds of motivation: however much they claim to work for the personal satisfaction they feel for a job well done, very few would continue to work if the salary were withdrawn. It is sometimes easy for a manager, who is mainly personally intrinsically motivated, to forget that others may not be and to forget to communicate appropriately with the more junior staff to keep them motivated. Doing so constitutes, in part, staff development.

An essential step in motivating staff is to ensure that they understand the purpose of the particular job they are doing and how this job well done contributes to the overall success of the organisation's goals. The importance of small contributions to overall success has long been acknowledged in the proverbial rhyme, 'For the want of a nail'.[1] When staff realise the extent of the potential effect of relatively minor actions, they see that they are important. The added benefit it that they can be trusted to perform something accurately: if the manager or supervisor has to closely check *everything* the junior staff do, it is a waste of time delegating it. Properly motivated staff should not, and do not, need constant close supervision. The other great motivator, personal benefits, can translate into various rewards; the one which should always be forthcoming, without any ulterior motive, is thanks and praise. This is part of the more general concept of treating people in the workplace with respect, an area which is attracting growing attention. In Canada, the Commission des normes de travail recently even launched a campaign calling for respect in the workplace, with the slogan, 'Au travail, employez le respect'[2] (Cartier Comunication, 2010).

While we all enjoy being treated with respect and appreciation, there is also the point of view which says, 'Give me compliments I can spend'. It is rarely within the gift of library managers to pay cash bonuses but there are other benefits more tangible than praise: being in line for a promotion or the opportunity to have some study time towards a further qualification, even a first class reference when they apply for a job elsewhere. Finally, it is desirable for management to demonstrate their own motivation and enthusiasm for the organisation's mission. Just as, in the classroom, learners respond positively to a good enthusiastic teacher, so too do employees respond to a dynamic leader.

Damage caused by lack of staff development

The quality of an organisation's staff can make or break its reputation. The return from capital expenditure on buildings and equipment may be severely diminished if misused or not fully realised by staff who have not been sufficiently trained. I have witnessed an incident when the assistive technology equipment, acquired to aid disabled readers, was not available to such a reader because the *one* person on the staff who knew how to use it was on holiday; in effect the money spent on the equipment had been wasted, as far as this user was concerned, and the self esteem of the staff who had not been trained to help was not enhanced either.

Internal to the library service, the value of staff development cannot be overstressed. Sometimes the staff development budget is in danger of only being available to the upper echelons of library staff. We would do well to remember that many user interactions take place with junior members of staff, who are often not qualified librarians. Do we value these staff sufficiently to keep them properly trained and informed of current events? Peters and Waterman (1995) emphasised the crucial importance of good frontline staff. No organisation creates a favourable impression if the frontline staff, particularly in the self-styled hub of information, the library, do not have a clear idea of the institution's organisation or any major events taking place. I have witnessed visitors, who have lost their way to an event on another part of the campus, call into a library to ask for the location of the event, only to be told that the library reception staff have no knowledge of the event, *because nobody thought of telling them*. This does not create a favourable impression of the library or indeed of the institution and does little for the self esteem or job satisfaction of the staff in question. The impressions, positive or negative, created by frontline staff resound much further than the initial interaction and the actual *cost* of keeping staff informed is minimal, especially if they have access to e-mail or an intranet.

Promoting from within the service

Additionally, frontline staff with the right personal qualities may well be a source of future professional staff. Many large commercial organisations, e.g. McDonald's, have a policy of promoting from within, with several benefits: the employer has had the opportunity of seeing the employee in the work situation, the employee will probably feel more positively motivated if their horizon is wider and, if they do rise through the ranks, will have a wealth of first-hand experience on which to draw in their dealings with junior staff. Many of the best librarians I know started their library careers as counter assistants. It is also motivating for the rest of the staff to see a colleague succeed, as an indication that effort is rewarded. It is recognised that not all more senior appointments should be made from within; sometimes it is appropriate to take on some fresh blood and ideas to keep the organisation vibrant.

Good personal qualities for staff

For all library staff, besides the need for being well-informed, the importance of good interpersonal skills cannot be over-stressed. Just as memories of positive encounters remain, so do those of negative ones. Libraries need staff with excellent technical and interpersonal skills, both of which can be improved by training. The desirable *personal qualities* for information professionals have already received some attention in a Library and Information Commission-funded research project, 'Likely to succeed: attitudes and aptitudes for an effective information profession for the 21st Century' (Library and Information Commission, 1998). In a national survey conducted across different library sectors and involving 439 respondents with an average of 22 years in the profession, respondents were asked to state the qualities which they deemed to be *most lacking* in new graduates and these included those of being *friendly, flexible and confident in own ability.* Even allowing for the seasoned professionals' possibly jaundiced view of the young, in view of the growing role of the librarian as teacher/facilitator/fellow explorer of new information horizons, it is not encouraging that new graduates were seen in such negative terms by their more experienced colleagues. End-users do rate the *friendliness and approachability* of staff quite highly: a male under-graduate, when asked to recall any abiding memories of using the public library service as a child, replied,

> I remember particularly one librarian who everybody commented on. She was the most sour-faced unfriendly woman on the face of the planet. If you wanted to take a book out it was like you had committed a mortal sin! (Hull, 2000)

We should remind counter staff that it is largely *they* who set the initial tone of the customer interface. Referring to counter staff in a university library, a female undergraduate reported: 'I've worked in the shop industry for 4 years and I know how to treat a customer. Some of them [counter staff] are OK but some of them are really miserable. They could smile at least ... I think a qualification for being a librarian must be to be miserable!' (Hull, 2000). The paramount importance of the staff/customer interface is also recognised by Millson-Martula and Menon (1995) who make the recommendation that: 'Hiring officials should make a concerted effort to employ frontline staff who possess excellent interpersonal skills together with a strong service orientation. For continuing staff, managers have the obligation to provide the proper training that will result in enhanced service.' Internally, is there scope for strengthening links with our colleagues on the front line? Without deluging them with too much detail, can we include them more in knowledge of the broader issues within the organisation? Do we always remember to express our own appreciation for their efforts and to give them a share of bouquets we, as more senior staff sometimes receive? Our junior staff, like our clients, are human and need and do appreciate praise for a job well done. It need not cost the earth: I still remember with positive feelings, X years later, the chief librarian who bought cream cakes for everyone on the library staff, following the award of an excellent rating on an institutional visit (and I haven't got a sweet tooth!). Of course it was no real recompense for the hard work we had put in, but it did show that it was appreciated.

The Barriers to Libraries research sample (Hull, 2000), while generally not *critical* of staff, did express a perception that their availability was insufficient and that they were frequently working under pressure. As one mature student summed up, 'It seemed there were never enough staff. They always seemed quite stressed out. It was OK if you got them on a good day.'

Quite rightly, the need for constant updating of *technical* skills is generally recognised. However, library staff may also need awareness-raising, or even refreshing, on some users' possible lack of previous experience in information retrieval matters, and their feelings of unease in alien surroundings.

Employing volunteers

There is a growing trend for libraries, in the interest of economy, to employ either volunteers or, in some college or university libraries, paid student workers.

This can be problematical in the case of volunteers, as those supervising them may feel that they cannot complain if the work is not done exactly as required: after all, their work is free, isn't it? The problem is akin to that experienced by a charity when well-meaning individuals used to donate their unwanted, and unsalable, goods which the charity then had the problem of disposing of. Most charities are now quite clear on specifying the type and condition of the goods they are willing to accept. Libraries can have the same problem re donated books and many, quite rightly, have developed very tight policies on donations. As I reflect on my days as a less experienced librarian, I wish that I had had a stricter policy in place at that time! It would have saved a lot of time and effort. The same principle applies to donated time. Volunteers should go through the same recruitment and training processes as paid members of staff. If they *really* do want to be useful to the organisation, they should see that this will benefit its efficiency and be willing to comply. Besides, many volunteers use their unpaid experience as collateral when applying for a paid position, either within the organisation or elsewhere. If they have been treated in exactly the same way as 'normal' members of staff, there is no ethical dilemma in giving them a 'normal' reference.

Junior staff need the bigger picture too

Employing students can be a way of benefiting the library and the individual student but their induction and training do need some careful thought. When part-time student advisors were first employed at Teesside University Library, besides patrolling and helping to maintain a quiet working environment, which they viewed as a negative role, they were also given the role of dealing with Level 1 enquiries, e.g. where are the photocopiers? what time does the library close on Sunday? etc. After they had been in post a short time, some of them, in attempting helpfulness, were observed attempting to answer queries far beyond their remit. They were quite obviously unclear as to how far their role should extend and an additional training session was arranged. They were given a talk by one of the Subject Team Leaders,

> outlining L&IS practice of working in teams, with each team respecting the acknowledged expertise of other teams and of 'referring on' where this will provide the customer with the best service. Another factor, to which permanent members of L&IS staff are sensitised, is that vague general queries often mask an inability to articulate a specific query, which may need 'unpacking' in a reference interview. The inexperienced worker may answer such a query *literally* without realising that the customer's needs have not been fulfilled. It was explained

to participants that librarianship is a graduate profession and that they were not expected to know as much as the professionals and that, indeed, no-one in L&IS has *all* the answers. (Hull and Oliver, 2003)

The comments received in the feedback on the session indicated that the student employees had *not* initially been clear on the exact definition of level 1 enquiries. Here are some of them: 'Everyone was made aware of the procedures that need to be followed', 'We are now able to see/recognise senior staff', 'We now all understand where we stand. And I strongly agree the procedure and feel comfortable working as a part of the team', 'It made me understand why people sit at the desk and your job roles', 'It helped us to gain an understanding of what queries should be dealt with by us and which ones should be passed on' (Hull and Oliver, 2003). If they had not been sure about their role, why had they not asked? Possibly because they did not want to appear stupid and thought everybody else seemed to understand, or maybe they were afraid they might lose the job. This was an example of how a cross-team staff development session can improve the communication between teams (the Academic Information Team and the Counter Services Team of which the student workers formed a part) and it certainly improved the service: from the very next day student workers referred on enquiries appropriately, some actually leading enquirers to the Information Desk, where they could get the more advanced help they needed.

This above example throws into relief the need for all members of staff to have an overview of the whole picture, so that they can appreciate where their role fits and how performing their role well assists the overall success of the library; in addition it is useful for everyone to be aware of the broader issues concerning the library's client group, whether it is a college, university or community. For example, if a large group of overseas students has just been recruited the desk staff will be alerted that they may have to be extra patient and remember to speak more slowly and clearly.

Although the underlying research has recently been reinterpreted with less marked results, the 'Hawthorne' effect should also be considered. The name is derived from the experiments to increase productivity at the Hawthorne Works plant of Western Electric. It was found that productivity increased in both the experimental group and the control group and the conclusion was drawn that the personnel increased productivity because someone was taking an interest in them, not because of any actual change in their working conditions. The studies showed that, although an individual's output is affected by their mental and physical potential, they are strongly influenced by social factors, and the relations that supervisors develop with workers tend to influence the manner in which the workers carry out directives (Franke and Kaul, 1978).

Recognising individual members of staff

Man is naturally a sociable animal. Everybody needs to be acknowledged as a person. At the extreme end of the scale, the most painful experience imaginable for a member of a work group would be to be 'sent to Coventry'.[3] Most human beings feel more secure and positive as part of a group where they are appreciated as an individual and their skills and positive attributes recognised. This is true for staff at all levels but especially those staff at the coal face who may have to deal politely with difficult or stressed customers on a regular basis.

Staff need to be kept up to date on practical day to day events and developments, either by very short team briefing sessions or by accessing e-mail or intranet sites at the start of each working session. But there is also a need for deeper communication between staff on different teams and at different levels in the library. It is therefore suggested that staff meetings for all staff should take place on a regular basis, not the ritualistic type where everyone mainly listens to the chairman, but an interactive one, where staff at every level are encouraged to contribute, to be held say once a month. More junior staff often have excellent ideas for improving the service, for two reasons: first, in many respects they are closer to the client groups as they often encounter more of them more frequently on a daily basis and can pick up on potential barriers; second, they may well have a less cluttered view of the situation, unlike senior management which is trying to juggle X number of variables simultaneously. We should show our appreciation for all staff suggestions for improvements, in pursuit of our service's strategic goals, even if it is decided not to implement them. It is a strange phenomenon that many library assistants, in the UK at least, are over-qualified for their actual job description; I have been in libraries where more than one has been a qualified teacher, surely a person already sensitised to perceive whether the user/resource interface is working as it should. It is a mistake to pigeonhole a person by their current situation: people are much more prepared to listen to the ideas of a person once they have been awarded a PhD, although these *very same* ideas had previously been dismissed as not worth listening to. Potential talent and original ideas may emerge in many places.

Our staff are, or should be, our greatest asset so let us treat them with respect, keep them updated and communicate with them. Good communications internal to the library are likely to foster good communications with external colleagues and partners.

Notes

1. For the want of a nail the shoe was lost, For the want of a shoe the horse was lost, For the want of a horse the rider was lost, For the want of a rider the battle was lost, For the want of a battle the kingdom was lost, And all for the want of a horseshoe nail.
2. Everyone deserves respect at work.
3. To be ignored or ostracised. The other group members pretend that the shunned person, although conspicuously present, cannot be seen or heard.

References

Cartier Communication (2010) available at *www .agencecartier.com/en/press/?n=58* (accessed 23/01/10).

Franke, R.H. and Kaul, J.D. (1978) 'The Hawthorne experiments: First statistical interpretation', *American Sociological Review*, 1978, 43, pp. 623–43.

Hull, B. (1997) 'Changes in the self concepts of adult students with special reference to previous educational disadvantage', University of Leeds (unpublished PhD).

Hull, B. (2000) 'Barriers to Libraries as agents of lifelong learning', London: Library and Information Commission, available at *http://lis.tees.ac.uk/research/researchbh.cfm* (accessed 23/09/10).

Hull, B. and Oliver, J. (2003) 'Training students to work in the learning resource centre', *SCONUL Newsletter*, Spring 2003, pp. 58–61.

Library and Information Commission (1998) 'Likely to succeed: attitudes and aptitudes for an effective information profession for the 21st Century', London: Library and Information Commission, available at *www.lboro.ac.uk/ departments/dils/Research/sucdesc.html*.

Millson-Martula, C. and Menon, V. (1995) 'Customer expectations: concepts and reality for academic library services', *College and Research Libraries*, January 1995, 33–47.

Peters, T. and Waterman, R.H. (1995) *In search of excellence. Lessons from America's best-run companies*, London: Harper Collins Business.

14

Self publicise

Abstract: This chapter considers various reasons underpinning the need for libraries and librarians to practise self promotion: to inform potential users, to forge links with the communities they serve, to become names with faces and to increase their chances of survival.

Key words: library publicity, library promotion, community links, liaison links, names and faces.

Bescheidenheit ist eine Zier
doch weiter kommt man ohne ihr.[1]

Sell your service!

As we saw in the chapter on images of librarians, information science/librarianship is greatly underestimated by the uninformed. Are we, as librarians, partly to blame? We live in a world where others constantly engage in continuous self-promotion. Are we in danger of being overlooked and undervalued unless we too engage in what could be seen as 'stating the obvious'? We know we have enormous skills, we provide access to treasure stores of information and culture and we are here waiting to help to change the world. But unless we communicate these facts clearly and constantly, we are in danger of not receiving due recognition: 'Libraries have made the grave mistake of assuming everyone knows how important they are' (Keller, 2008).

Are we perhaps afraid of being accused of wasting resources on advertising? If we look at the business world we see that advertising, in consumers' eyes, is often an indication of added value and that 'this cost perception evokes an inference about brand quality. Perceived advertising costs might evoke quality inferences for several reasons: (1) perceived costs may act as a signal of a manufacturer's advertising effort, which indicates managerial confidence in the product; (2) consumers may perceive a correlation between advertising costs and product quality (Kirmani, 1990).

It is sad but true that there is a human tendency to underappreciate something which is not trumpeted. Many years ago, in the heyday of liberal Adult Education courses in the UK, the city of Manchester organised a scheme whereby, for a single annual payment of £10, an individual could enrol for as many Adult Education courses as they wanted. The tutors were well qualified and the courses professionally conceived. The scheme was discontinued after one year, not because of an oversubscription but because there was a huge demand at enrolment, followed by a rapid falling off in subsequent weeks; when dropouts were asked about their failure to continue, they intimated that they did not think that it mattered, the courses were so cheap, weren't they? Unfortunately for many there is a real confusion between price and value, so it is sometimes worthwhile using a little trickery to stimulate some appreciation. When I used to conduct information literacy sessions on the use of subscription databases, I was frequently disappointed by the subsequent relatively low usage of the databases when the monthly statistics were checked. After I started telling them how much the databases cost, and that they, as students, were privileged in having access, the monthly usage increased noticeably.

On a similar note, I also started including some facts and figures on budget, opening hours, number of loans, etc. into general induction sessions, presented as a kind of 'sales pitch'. It is rather sad that this should be necessary but it is.

In the Barriers to Libraries Project (Hull, 2000) an unacceptably large percentage of students (over 40 per cent) reported non-attendance at LRC [Library] induction sessions. Evidently, this is indicative of a lack of awareness of the centrality of the library to the student learning experience, as failure to attend has a statistically significant correlation with agreement with the statement, 'I didn't realise that learning how to use the LRC [Library] was part of being a student.' This clearly indicates the need for greater recognition of the importance of Information Literacy at the institutional level and more self-promotion by the library.

The need to remind users

One key role for librarians is to constantly promote new sources and refresh customers on the usefulness of existing ones. We may fall into the trap of believing that we have already advertised the new database, the special collection or our user education sessions. But if we look to the world of business, we see that the brand leader does not stop advertising on the assumption that everyone already knows about the product or service. It is recognised that even existing customers need reminding of what is available and there are always potentially new customers out there. In speaking of the need for continual promotion, an advertising guru reminded us a long time ago: 'You can never wash the dinner dishes and say they are done. You have to keep doing them constantly' (Lawrence, 1966). The quote *is* old;

although we are nowadays less likely to actually wash the dinner dishes ourselves, the dishwasher still needs to be loaded! Librarians would do well to take this to heart. For those working in academic libraries there is a constant influx of new students, some from countries with completely different library systems and ethos. Public librarians could see their client group as more static, but they have potential access to the life blood of future library users – children! Amazingly, quite a large number of children in Wales were woefully ignorant about the services available to them at the library:

> The National Marketing Strategy survey for libraries in Wales found many children believed they had to pay to borrow books.
> ... A lot of people who don't use libraries have a very negative view of them and don't think they are relevant to them ... No one has looked at marketing libraries as a national brand before. I think the survey findings were a surprise to everyone because if you talk to people who use libraries they tend to be very happy with the service they get. (Wightwick, 2007)

There is evidence that librarians are beginning to realise that their survival may well depend on learning to self publicise more. The Chartered Institute of Library and Information Professionals (CILIP) has issued very practical guides to marketing libraries, and uses the Chartered Institute of Marketing's definition that marketing is 'the management process responsible for identifying, anticipating and satisfying customer requirements profitably', adding the rider 'There is tendency to assume "profitably" equates only to money. It is possible to profit in a non-financial way; you profit if you gain a benefit or advantage. So, for instance, an organisation may profit through raising awareness of an issue' (CILIP, 2009).

Integrating into your community

All libraries serve a community or client group, and to do their job really well need to be a fully integrated part of that group; this can offer opportunities for some 'stealth marketing' – usually seen as unethical, but in this case justifiable, considering that our motive is philanthropic, not monetary.

Satisfied users as ambassadors

Sometimes we inherit a library service which is poorly integrated. To mix metaphors, we know that Rome wasn't built in a day, but one of the best ways of raising our profile is with 'Trojan mice'! Each time we have a satisfied client, we have created a potential ambassador for our skills and services, especially if we gently enlist them as promoters of the library. Satisfied customers bring in more (Peters and Waterman, 1995). As Keller (2008) suggests, the value of the Royal Library of Alexandria was probably spread across the Mediterranean by satisfied customers. Sometimes contented clients might need a gentle hint that their word of mouth publicity could help the library's cause or even survival. It often does not occur to satisfied clients to mention their appreciation other than to verbally thank the person responsible. It is harder for funding bodies to make cuts in high profile institutions. Perhaps it is worth reviving the old tradesman's adage: 'If you're not satisfied, tell us. If you are satisfied, tell your friends.'

To use an analogy from a very different field, the manager of a breast cancer screening unit in the UK, on receipt of a letter of appreciation for the way the centre staff dealt with women in this vulnerable state, stated that such letters were kept on file and acted as valuable ammunition in the face of any threatened reduction in funding.

It is a truism that familiarity breeds friendship or at least co-operation. If the library staff are more visible in the community served by the library, they are more likely to be seen as full members of that community; the social psychology 'ingroup/outgroup' concept, whereby members of one's own group (the ingroup) are privileged over the outgroup, is quite powerful in parts of life. I hear of people dying in a plane crash and I am sorry, but even more sorry when I find they are from my country, and quite devastated when I discover they are from my home town and I even know one or two of them slightly. The ivory tower model of librarianship is not a useful one either for promoting the library or ensuring its survival.

Importance of names

A first step in becoming part of the ingroup is taking advantage of the face and name concept. People outside the library need to know who the library staff are, as we are more likely to liaise with people we know by sight and whose name we know: for a human being, nothing is worse than the Kafkaesque nightmare of anonymity: we tend to feel more comfortable and in control if we are interacting with a named individual. Human beings relate well to other human beings with *names*! We even go as far as anthropomorphising inanimate objects by giving them (usually women's) names: ships, cars, on Italian railways even trains are given names.

If they are so important to the human psyche, we should take full advantage of this by making sure people know who we are and by using other people's names as far as we can. When I appeared and was named on a library induction video it was somewhat disconcerting to be greeted by name by numerous people across campus, whom I had not previously formally met, and so could not salute them by name. But at least they knew who I was and I was half-way to knowing them! I was not just a name without a face, or a face without a name. Recognising the importance of others' names brings with it the burden of remembering them. There are lots of tricks to remembering: in a large gathering, where you are meeting a huge number of people for the first time, a committee meeting or a new class of students, I have found it useful to add a note next to every name of how each one seems different to me which gives me a personal tag for my memory, e.g. 'fantastic black hair', or 'Johnny Depp' or even 'Aunt Teresa', if she reminds me of my maiden aunt! People are often surprised at how quickly you have learned their names and take this as a compliment – that you are interested. A word of warning: don't leave the list on view! I dread to think what shorthand might appear against my name on a list ...

A trick for eliciting a name that you have forgotten and still retain some credibility is to ask them to remind you. If they answer 'John Smith' your answer is 'Yes, I know your name's John. I'd just forgotten your surname' or 'Yes, I know your name is Smith. I'd just forgotten your first name'. Not perfect, but it does allow us to partially extricate ourselves from an embarrassing situation.

The naming idea is utilised in many areas outside libraries: the use of name badges, say at conferences, helps lubricate the wheels of communication, making it easier for us to approach someone without a formal introduction; the telephone sales pitch often starts with the caller trying to personalise the interaction by telling us their name, although this is rarely sufficient to compensate for their invasion of our privacy.

Joining in

Another useful device for getting known outside the confines of the library is to join in the social life of your institution or community. Being seen as a 'team player', either literally on the football team or metaphorically on the fundraising for charity committee, firmly integrates you, as the librarian, and subconsciously the library itself into the wider community.

Publicise your achievements

How do we librarians in universities and colleges gain recognition from our institutional academic colleagues: recognition that we too are experts in our own field of information handling, that we are different but equal? McNicol (2003) observed that 'research can serve a number of practical purposes' including 'raising the profile of libraries'. Librarians *do* conduct and publish research and, as reflective practitioners, we frequently act on that research to make changes to our service provision. Do we bother to make our academic colleagues aware of this? Learning resources are at the very heart of lifelong learning. Do we make efforts to publicise our research findings *outside of* our own specialist LIS circles? The research findings from 'Barriers to Libraries as agents of lifelong learning' research project (Hull, 2000), for example, besides being widely disseminated to LIS professionals in conferences and publications, have also been publicised in adult and continuing education[2] and computer ethics circles,[3] thus making them available to those who would not normally be aware that information professionals conduct research and endeavour to act on its findings. Sometimes when a librarian presents a paper at a conference for another discipline, the reactions of other participants can be interesting: for some the librarian is the 'joker in the pack' but for others it can be a first step in seeing librarians in a totally different light. I have even made unexpectedly useful contacts with other libraries through these non-librarian contacts at conferences. Perhaps most importantly, spending time with a professional group of non-librarians offers a frank insight into how information workers are perceived by the communities they serve: it is not always flattering.

There are many challenges that remain for librarians in today's uncertain times. If we are to succeed in this changing environment, there are some key factors to bear in mind. First, it pays to advertise! Let's polish up our trumpets and remind people that we are experts in our field. Second, even in this electronic age the most satisfying interface is human. Let us remember that we are dealing with people. Finally, alliances can improve our prestige and influence. Time spent creating links with others in our wider community is usually time well spent.

Notes

1. Old German proverb, loosely translates as, 'Modesty is a wonderful thing, but you go a lot further without it'.
2. E.g. FACE conferences. See *http://www.f-a-c-e.org.uk/* (accessed 16/01/2011).
3. E.g. Ethicomp conferences. See *http://www.ccsr.cse.dmu.ac.uk/* (accessed 16/01/2011).

References

CILIP (2009) 'Practical Guide: Marketing Your Library & Information Service (Part 1)', available at *www.cilip.org. uk/membership/benefits/informed/practical-guides/pages/ marketing.aspx*.

Keller, J.A. (2008) 'Branding and Marketing your Library', *Public Libraries*, September/October, pp. 45–51.

Kirmani, A. (1990) 'The effect of perceived advertising cost on brand perceptions', *The Journal of Consumer Research*, 17, 2, pp. 160–71.

Lawrence, M.W. (1966) 'On need for fresh approaches', *Time*, 3 October 1966.

McNicol, S. (2003) 'Research in academic libraries: a survey of practitioners', *SCONUL Newsletter*, 29, pp. 4–8.

Peters, T. and Waterman, R.H. (1995) *In search of excellence. Lessons from America's best-run companies*, London: Harper Collins Business.

Wightwick, A. (2007) 'We can't afford to use libraries, children think', *Western Mail* (Cardiff, Wales), 19 April 2007.

15

Breaking down the library walls: responding to the needs of the Google generation

Denise Turner

Abstract: Changes in technology and availability of information online bring both challenges and opportunities. How can librarians change their practice and respond to the needs of a generation who have grown up with the Internet? This chapter presents two case studies focusing on initiatives to break down some of the barriers students face in developing information literacy.

Key words: embedded librarians, critical thinking, outreach, roving.

New technology provides many opportunities to support students virtually. It could be argued that a generation who have grown up with the Internet no longer require face to face help from librarians. Instead a pilot service at Teesside University used the potential of technology to free librarians from the information desk, to proactively invite face to face enquiries outside the walls of the library. The first case study discusses the Librarians2U initiative and identifies some critical factors for success. The second case study presents one approach to teaching critical thinking skills. In a constantly changing information environment it is vital that students are information literate and able not only to find information but to evaluate it and use it ethically. Librarians face barriers in teaching these skills when learners believe they are already proficient searchers able to easily find the information they need. The critical thinking tool discussed aims to engage students in a critical thinking exercise and to reflect on their own practice. Both case studies are examples of librarians adapting to the needs of a new generation and changing their own practice.

The following case study evaluates a trial service to provide outreach services to students and staff within their academic school.

Background project 1

In recent years, there has been an increasing demand for librarians at Teesside University to provide workshops to introduce students to the resources available for their subject area. These 'one shot' sessions are normally frontloaded into the curriculum and some students may fail to recognise their significance. If academic staff do not signpost the importance of these workshops, some students view them as optional. However, later in their programme students regret not having taken the opportunity that was offered to them (Hull, Turner and Martin, 2002).

Following feedback from students, one to one sessions to offer support at the time of need were introduced to capitalise on these 'teachable moments'. Despite initial misgivings that librarians would be overwhelmed, the actual take up was fairly low. Bookings may have been affected by the timing of the sessions or the availability of other avenues to seek advice. However, tutors' comments evidenced that they had actively encouraged some students to book an appointment with a librarian but only a small number of students appeared to do so. Research on library anxiety (Mellon, 1986) suggests that some students see their lack of knowledge as a source of shame. Students felt that they alone did not possess the requisite skills to use the library, viewing the library as unwelcoming. This fear and uncertainty may cause students to view their questions as trivial, especially faced with library staff who appear to have more important things to do (Robinson and Reid, 2007; Durrance, 1995). Robinson (2007) revealed that students are unsure about the type of question that they can ask and so turn to peers rather than approaching staff (Robinson and Reid, 2007; Alexitch, 2002; Moore and Wells, 2009). Some students may view seeking help as a sign of failure (Karabenick and Knapp, 1991). However, once barriers to seeking help are removed, there is evidence that students do value face to face support from librarians (Johnson, 2004; Robinson and Reid, 2007; Ismail, 2010). Given the importance of dialogue to support learning (Laurillard, 2001), how can we break down these perceived barriers?

Librarians at Teesside University are already utilising social media services to communicate with students in the online environment. However, using the availability of online resources so that librarians can be available to students in social spaces outside the library had not been considered. A review of the literature found little published research but subsequent searches (using terms such as 'embedded', 'outreach' and 'roving') demonstrated that many librarians were already exploring other methods to engage with students beyond the library walls. Some librarians had done this through necessity (Arendt, 2006); others made use of existing peer support networks (Ruediger and Neal, 2004). There were some who wanted to explore the potential of offering services in non traditional settings within the University (Nims, 1998; Kuchi, Mullen and Tama-Bartels,

2004). Bosque and Chapman (2007) provide a good overview of this type of outreach.

Pilot service: discussion

Following discussion with colleagues a decision was made to use the foyer of the School of Social Sciences and Law for a pilot service. The area is wireless enabled and already used by academic tutors from the School to provide tutorial support to students. The librarians worked closely with key academic staff within the School to determine the best time to offer the service. The Librarians2U pilot ran every Monday and Tuesday (11–12 noon) from 11 January 2010 until 23 March 2010. This time frame was chosen to coincide with a period when students were preparing for assessment. Sessions were advertised using a variety of methods:

- E-mail to all academic staff in SSSL
- Announcements in lectures
- Notices on the virtual learning environment
- Flyers on tables in the area chosen for the pilot
- Front page news on the library web site
- Notices on TV screens in the School of Social Sciences and Law

Information used to advertise the sessions gave the time when a librarian would be available; students who could not attend were advised to book one to one sessions at a time of their choice. Publicity material illustrated example questions to normalise the need for additional support. Rather than sit behind a desk, the librarian sat with the students. To identify the location of the librarian there was a small sign and laptop displaying the Librarians2U logo.

During the pilot, the three librarians involved kept a journal recording the number and type of enquiries, notes about how busy the area was and any reflections on how the service could be improved. Analysis of the journal showed that, in total, librarians answered questions from 31 students. The majority of questions were related to academic work (e.g. finding journal articles, referencing) or use of library services. A few questions were about using the virtual learning environment. Although advertising was directed exclusively at students in Social Sciences and Law, four students from other academic schools attended sessions. Outside these times, 26 students booked a one to one session with a librarian, compared with only six students during the same time period the previous year. As the service was aimed at students, the benefits to academic staff of having librarians easily available had not been considered, but analysis of the journal showed that in addition to the students there were 23 enquiries from academic staff. Some commented on what an excellent idea Librarians2U was and used the opportunity to directly refer students to the librarian for help. Recently published research demonstrates how useful outreach to academic staff can be (Watson, 2010).

Several limitations to this pilot study need to be acknowledged, particularly the short timescale. The aim of the pilot service was to assess potential demand. Based on the trial and from researching the literature there are a number of significant factors to be considered if this type of service is to succeed.

Choosing the right location has an impact on the success of the service. 'A high-traffic area is essential' (Wagner, 2004) and the nature of the space chosen is important. The foyer used for the pilot service was already used by tutors to offer tutorials, so there was no sense of librarians invading a space that students viewed as purely social. Increased visibility of librarians reinforced our role in supporting not just students but academic staff. Both groups made use of the service to ask their questions. In future a large banner behind the librarian will be used as a visible indicator that the service is available.

The limited nature of the trial meant that the librarians were only available to a fraction of students. At least one student travelled in specifically to talk to the Librarians2U and one of the younger students admitted to preferring to talk to a familiar face. Advertising was targeted at Social Sciences and Law students, so it was surprising to attract students from other Schools. Why were some students specifically seeking out the librarians when this service is already available from Information Desks in the library? Was it because the examples of questions communicated a clear message about what support was on offer? Do we clearly communicate support available from information desks or expect that students will already know?

An experiment with this type of service by a librarian at Ann Arbor University illustrates that timing is key (Frierson, 2007). The idea for the sessions came from first year student feedback but the needs of other students and staff should have been considered when planning the service. Ideally this service would be run across a whole year to determine the peak demand periods, but with such a small team this is currently not possible.

Close liaison with key members of academic staff ensured that there was support for this new service at all levels. There is demand for the service to continue from the senior management within the School and they have approached other support departments to provide the same type of service as Librarians2U. For example, careers advice staff will now be offering a drop-in service from the same foyer. What is particularly interesting is that the careers advice centre is already physically close to the foyer.

This year the Librarians2U service will be rolled out to other academic schools. Our vision is to break down barriers that stop some students fulfilling their true potential. Librarians2U made librarians highly visible and approachable, removing some psychological barriers to seeking help. Although the actual time librarians were available in the foyer was short, it sent out a clear message about our role. It is vital that we continue to explore ways to break down barriers and to create services that actively invite enquiries as without our support some learners may simply give up (Hull, 2000).

The following case study describes and evaluates the design and implementation of a learning object developed to be used as a tool to test critical thinking skills.

Background project 2

An increasing reliance on search engines like Google requires highly developed critical thinking skills in order to navigate a sea of information that lacks the rigorous editorial processes of scholarly literature. Research by OCLC (De Rosa et al., 2006) found that 89 per cent of students began their search for information with a search engine, while only 2 per cent started from their library website. Findings were consistent with the Google Generation report (Rowlands, Nicholas and Williams, 2008) which discovered a reluctance to use library sponsored content combined with overconfidence in a search engine's ability to find quality information. When faced with a list of results, young people tend to:

Move rapidly from page to page, spending little time reading or digesting information, and they have difficulty making relevance judgements about the pages they retrieve. (Rowlands, Nicholas and Williams, 2008, p. 297)

An issue for educators trying to engage students with these skills is that they simply do not recognise the need for them and overestimate their own performance, effectively creating a barrier to their own learning:

There is a big gap between their actual performance in information literacy skills tests and their self estimates of information skills and library anxiety. (Rowlands, Nicholas and Williams, 2008, p. 303)

Assessing the credibility of information found on the Internet remains an essential skill and one that students appear to lack, despite increased exposure to the Internet. Many research studies (Flanagin and Metzge, 2007) have examined how users critically evaluate information, but only a few have actually observed user behaviour. The researcher and a colleague decided to use the findings from the Google Generation study to inform their work by introducing material on critical thinking skills to a group of learners.

The group of learners that were identified to pilot this material were studying a summer voluntary module called 'Preparing for your dissertation', taught partly by librarians. The module focuses on compiling a bibliography for a piece of research and aims to give final year undergraduate students lots of practical experience of searching the literature. The diverse range of dissertation topics and the increasingly complex range of information sources available, mean that even with six hours delivery time there is little room for additional content. The use of Internet sources was already part of the content and class discussions showed that students could often articulate relevant evaluation criteria. However, bibliographies on their chosen topic, which form part of the assessment, suggest that they do not apply these criteria in practice. Research for material on critical thinking skills to enrich the module content did not reveal anything that could be utilised, as the material identified was either aimed at a younger audience or was too detailed for the time available.

Implementation and pilot testing

The researcher worked with a colleague (Sue Myer) to develop and test a critical thinking tool that could be piloted with this group and shared with the academic community. The tool is based on constructivist principles, presenting learners with an authentic scenario and building on the critical thinking skills that they already have. It aims to provide learners with immediate feedback, be engaging and fun. Developed for a generation that have grown up with the Internet, the tool uses common web conventions used by services such as Amazon and YouTube to obtain users ratings. As learners in the pilot group came from diverse subject areas a generic scenario was chosen that it was hoped students could relate to. Learners are presented with a screen showing three extracts of information found from a search about the dangers of mobile phones. Their task is straight-forward: from this information alone, they simply give each extract a star rating based on its usefulness for an academic essay about mobile phones. The extracts are carefully chosen and all appear relevant to the topic, but their origins are very different. One extract is from a peer reviewed journal, one from a magazine and the final extract is from a website that is trying to sell a product. Faced with such a brief extract, how can learners evaluate the quality of the information? Yet this is exactly the way that search engines display results: with few clues about the original source of the information, learners are forced to make choices based on relevance alone.

Once learners have voted, the next screen reveals the bibliographic citation for each extract. The screen also shows the rating given on the previous screen and allows learners to reassess their rating based on the additional information about the source. The developers hypothesised that votes for the website will be lower at this stage, but that students would struggle to identify the peer reviewed source based on this information alone.

On the next screen the citation becomes a link and students are encouraged to visit each of the sources before making their final assessment. Below each extract is a complete history of the rating previously given, providing a visual representation of how thinking has developed. Visiting the links should make it easy for students to identify the most authoritative source. The final screen shows both the learners rating for each source and the rating of an expert and discusses the factors considered to arrive at the expert rating. This gives the learner immediate feedback and allows them to compare their thought process with that of an expert.

The critical thinking tool was piloted with 34 students from a range of disciplines who were studying the module discussed earlier. The assessment for this module is a workbook in which one question asks students to reflect on their learning from the critical thinking task. Reflecting on concrete experience is a necessary stage for effective learning (Fry, Ketteridge and Marshall, 2009, p. 15) and this worked well as a method of evaluating the critical thinking tool. Learners' comments showed that it really made them think about the way they evaluated information:

The task was extremely enlightening as it made me question my response to the material I research. While generally I rated them appropriately I was way off on the first extract as I was misled by the reference that looked promising. It has definitely opened my eyes and made me think to really scrutinise my research and its sources.

Other students talked about the importance of checking for bias, looking at the evidence base and the need to view quotations in their original context. For some students it made them reassess their approach to using information from the web and was a 'quick lesson learnt'; for others it affirmed that they had correctly evaluated the extracts: 'felt like an advert from the start, glad I stayed with this thought as my ratings equal to exercise rating'.

Conclusion

Following the pilot, the critical thinking tool was made available on the library website (*http://lis.tees.ac.uk/infoskills_gen/critical/exercise.cfm*) and over the last 12 months has been visited nearly 800 times. Requests from academic staff have led to the development of some subject specific versions, plus all students in the School of Social Sciences and Law at Teesside University have a version of the exercise embedded into their modules on the VLE.

The critical thinking tool allows students to behave as they would in real life and gives them the opportunity to learn from their own behaviour. Many diagnostic tools ask students to rate their own ability but research by Ehrlinger et al. (2008) on competency theory reveals that underlying this approach is the belief that people have the metacognitive skills to do this. Ehrlinger believes that some people do not have these skills and will overestimate their abilities. This tool gives immediate and constructive feedback allowing the learner to compare their performance with that of an expert. Based on the theory of scaffolding learning, the feedback suggests factors that need to be considered when evaluating information. Links to materials aimed at further developing critical thinking are then presented to the learner. Our hope is that making students reflect on their actual performance, rather than asking for their subjective assessment, forces some students to reassess their competency and could remove this barrier to their learning.

References

Alexitch, L.R. (2002) 'The role of help-seeking attitudes and tendencies in students' preferences for academic advising', *Journal of College Student Development*, 43(1), 5–19.

Arendt, J. (2006) 'When the walls crash down: offer services where the students are', *College and Research Libraries News*, 67 (December), available at *http://opensiuc.lib.siu.edu/cgi/viewcontent.cgi?article=1006&context=morris_articles* (accessed 1/11/10).

Bosque, D.D. and Chapman, K. (2007) 'Your place or mine? Face-to-face reference services across campus', *New Library World*, 108(5), 247–62.

De Rosa, C., Cantrell, J., Hawk, J. and Wilson, A. (2006) *College students' perceptions of libraries and information resources*, Dublin, Ohio: OCLC Online Computer Library Center, available at *www.oclc.org/reports/2005perceptions.htm* (accessed 5/11/10).

Durrance, J. (1995) 'Factors that influence reference success:

what makes questioners willing to return?', *The Reference Librarian*, 23(49), 243–65.

Ehrlinger, J., Johnson, K., Banner, M., Dunning, D. and Kruger, J. (2008) 'Why the unskilled are unaware: further explorations of (absent) self-insight among the incompetent', *Organizational Behavior and Human Decision Processes*, 105(1), 98–121.

Flanagin, A. and Metzge, M. (2007) 'Bibliography on web/internet credibility', *University of California, Santa Barbara*, available at *www.credibility.ucsb.edu/files/web_credibility_bibliography.pdf* (accessed 26/10/10).

Frierson, E. (2007) 'Some librarian: librarian with a latte', available at *http://somelibrarian.blogspot.com/2007/04/librarian-with-latte.html* (accessed 15/10/10).

Fry, H., Ketteridge, S. and Marshall, S. (2009) *A Handbook for Teaching and Learning in Higher Education Enhancing Academic Practice*, 3rd edn, New York: Routledge.

Hull, B. (2000) 'Barriers to Libraries as agents of lifelong learning', London: Library and Information Commission, available at *http://lis.tees.ac.uk/research/researchbh.cfm* (accessed 15/10/10).

Hull, B., Turner, D. and Martin, L. (2002) 'Introducing first year psychology undergraduates to information handling: comparing two institutions', *Sconul Newsletter*, 27, 14–18.

Ismail, L. (2010) 'What net generation students really want: Determining library help-seeking preferences of undergraduates', *Reference Services Review*, 38(1), 10–27.

Johnson, C.M. (2004) 'Online chat reference: survey results from affiliates of two universities', *Reference User Services Quarterly*, 43(3), 237–47.

Karabenick, S.A, and Knapp, J.R. (1991) 'Relationship of academic help seeking to the use of learning strategies and other instrumental achievement behavior in college students', *Journal of Educational Psychology*, 83(2), 221–30.

Kuchi, T., Mullen, L.B. and Tama-Bartels, S. (2004) 'Librarians without borders: reaching out to students at a campus center', *Reference and User Services Quarterly*, 43(4), 310–18.

Laurillard, D. (2001) *Rethinking University Teaching: A Conversational Framework for the Effective Use of Learning Technologies*, 2nd edn, London: Routledge.

Mellon, C.A. (1986) 'Library anxiety: a grounded theory and its development', *College Research Libraries*, 47(March), 160–5.

Moore, A.C. and Wells, K.A. (2009) 'Connecting 24/5 to millennials: providing academic support services from a learning commons', *The Journal of Academic Librarianship*, 35(1), 75–85.

Nims, J. (1998) 'Meeting students on their own turf', *Research Strategies*, 16(1), 85–9.

Robinson, C.M. and Reid, P.H. (2007) 'Do academic enquiry services scare students?', *Reference Services Review*, 35(3), 405–24.

Rowlands, I., Nicholas, D. and Williams, P. (2008) 'The Google generation: the information behaviour of the researcher of the future', *Aslib Proceedings: New Information Perspectives*, 60(4), 290–310.

Ruediger, C. and Neal, S. (2004) 'Tapping into student networks', *College and Research Libraries News*, 65, 78–80.

Wagner, A.B. (2004) 'On-site reference services and outreach: setting up shop where our patrons live', Science & Engineering Library, Arts and Sciences Libraries, State University of New York at Buffalo, Paper presented to the Special Libraries Association National Meeting, 8 June 2004, Nashville, available at *www.acsu.buffalo*

.edu/~abwagner/Outreach-SLAPaper-2004.htm (accessed 15/10/10).

Watson, E. (2010) 'Taking the mountain to Mohammed: the effect of librarian visits to faculty members on their use of the library', *New Review of Academic Librarianship*, 16(2), 145–59.

16

Communication within partnerships at Deakin University Library: the liaison link

Christine Oughtred
and Marion Churkovich

Abstract: The role of liaison librarians, while not a new concept, is being re-energised and further developed within the university context. This chapter will look at three examples at Deakin University, Australia to highlight how positive communication can inform partnerships and improve outcomes.

Key words: role of liaison librarians, communication, partnerships within the university environment.

Introduction

Deakin University was established in 1977 as a new university offering a broad range of courses for rural and regional students and pioneering innovative teaching to off-campus and distance students. It has since become the fastest growing university in Australia, a multiple campus facility spread across Western Victoria and Melbourne, increasing its onshore student intake by 41 per cent in the last eight years.

The Deakin University Library has always been strongly committed to providing students and staff, whoever and wherever they are, access to high quality scholarly material and assistance at their point of need. The Library Liaison Service was established to facilitate this outcome, in other words to become the link between the library and its clients. Liaison Librarians have long been valued by students and academic staff for high levels of information literacy support, disseminating information about new products and resources, ensuring collection development is in line with curriculum changes and supports research needs, and actively seeking new ways of faculty interaction. A review of the liaison service in 2008 revealed a high level of satisfaction from its client base (Deakin University Library, 2009).

The importance of partnerships for library services has always been acknowledged and is well established in library literature (Rodwell and Fairbairn, 2008). The Deakin University Library Liaison service is a vital link in establishing effective partnerships with other areas of the University when time and resources are invested, flexibility negotiated, and trust established.

Changing university culture in Australia, such as new government targets for growth in student numbers including representation of equity groups,[1] the increasing time pressures on academic staff and the emphasis on research output has opened up new opportunities for the Library's support services to develop stronger partnerships within the University to add value. 'This means opening up practices to try different things, to take risks and to experiment' (Rodwell and Fairbairn, 2008: 121).

Exemplary library partnerships 'are built on shared understandings of how collective expertise can enhance student learning and research' (Doskatsch, 2003: 117). This is difficult to achieve through voicemail and e-mail.

Opportunities to meet face-to-face are needed 'to establish a sense of collegiality, an essential element of collaboration' (Doskatsch, 2003: 118). Recent Deakin experience of personalised communication between Liaison Librarians and staff in faculties, divisions and institutes has shown how much more can be achieved than through the traditional delivery of service.

The following three partnerships illustrate how communication has played a vital role in their effectiveness.

Librarian in residence

The Librarian in Residence (LIR) programme, where a liaison librarian is situated physically in the faculty, had its beginnings in 2007 when the Science Liaison Librarian based at Geelong campus was invited by a senior researcher to be 'on hand' each week for researchers at the newly developed Geelong Technical Precinct (GTP). The GTP isa specifically funded government initiative to enter into partnerships with enterprises from outside the university. His role was to provide assistance with literature and database searching, endnote, ordering and other library services.

This concept was then piloted in the Faculty of Business and Law at the Melbourne Campus in 2009 where a programme was initiated to embed librarians within the faculty for short periods each week to provide closer contact with faculty staff, especially in relation to supporting research needs. It was seen to be a way of building stronger partnerships and, as a result, the Business and Law liaison librarians received a nomination for Outstanding Contribution to the Faculty's Operational Plan in 2009 in recognition of the value of the programme. In 2010 this programme was rolled out to all campuses and faculties. Every liaison librarian involved in this programme records each communication transaction with staff to track the usage. These statistics will be used in a regular review and will inform change to the programme.

Our involvement in the Librarian in Residence programme for the Arts and Education faculty at the Geelong campus began this year in February 2010, just prior to the start of the academic year. As we job share this liaison position we decided to spend one morning each in the faculty. Our promotion consisted of a self produced A4 sheet with our photo taken together including details of when and where we would be in the faculty. The programme was promoted by a senior academic and we spent time door knocking to introduce our service. Our approach was to be available to academics in their offices at their point of need. We share space with other staff and researchers and have needed to change location several times in this short period, which has created extra promotional challenges.

Recently we sent an e-mail containing some questions requesting feedback from our campus based academic staff about this initiative. As it was nearing the end of the academic year we thought it was an appropriate time for reflection. The responses to one question in particular were very insightful and reinforced our own opinion of how the programme was working and the changing the nature of our relationships with our clients.

This question was: *What benefits (if any) can you identify from us being in the faculty?*

The responses confirmed our own supposition that perception of our role, personal relationships, visibility, research support and a collaborative approach have all improved since the introduction of Librarian in Residence.

Perception plays a key role in open communication as the statement below affirms:

> Perception is everything – and while you've always been accessible – this programme reinforces this idea and I believe is more likely to encourage staff to seek support etc. It certainly has had that effect for me.

Another aspect of our liaison work, which is changing, is the increase in the collaborative aspect of delivering information literacy programmes. After consultations with academic staff we have increased the amount of short presentations and given lectures on research skills. Increasingly these sessions came about through informal discussions and incidental conversations in the faculty staffroom.

As one academic commented: 'This has been a fortuitous conversation ... I would never have thought of this if we hadn't spoken here today.'

Personal relationships have also begun to change, as the statements below indicate. This also relates to staff understanding of our expertise and growing confidence to seek support.

> I've [sic] ... developed a better understanding about your role and how you may help me (for research and teaching) and my students.
>
> We [sic] Get to know you personally and build rapport. Makes it easier to ask for help etc. as I felt you belong to us.
>
> The fact that library staff are in the teaching environs creates a more relaxed, ongoing relationship – very positive one too.

A higher visibility has been an important outcome for our clients who have stated 'more and more communication/ cooperation takes place online or via e-mail': there is 'no substitute for face to face and breaking down of silos'.

We have also noticed an increase in the variety of research support requested since we started this programme: 'you can discuss our research needs and how they relate to library resources'.

Research training

Two Research librarian positions were created in 2009 to support the University's commitment to research. The University has developed strategic goals to establish Deakin in the top third of universities within Australia. Research features strongly in these initiatives. One in particular was the creation of the Institute of Research Training (IRT) to coordinate 'the support for higher degree by research candidates and early career researchers' (Deakin University, 2010).

The Research Librarians (based at two different campuses) established a connection with the Institute following their appointments in 2009. The Library recognised that although personalised assistance already existed for HDR students this needed to be extended to provide high-level support, including advanced in-depth research skills development (Lingham, 2010). New HDR students receive a welcome letter from the university librarian, followed by e-mail communication and if possible a face-to-face consultation with their liaison librarian to establish an ongoing relationship. It was seen by this group of library staff that to reach the maximum number of HDR students who are spread across campuses it was vital to integrate library training into the mainstream HDR programme run by IRT.

The library's role was considered to be essential to the institute's programme and the research librarians developed three workshops to be run every month and over multiple campuses as part of the overall HDR programme in 2010.

The sessions were tailored to whether participants were in the early, middle or late stages of candidature. The library sessions covered developing approaches to finding and evaluating information, showcasing research and the analysis process of discovering quality journals for potential publication. A third session covered in-depth training of storing references using the Endnote bibliographic software.

Each session had approximately 19 participants and from February until May 2010 this included a total of 230 students. They were run for all faculties, and liaison librarians became important as co-presenters. It was also a good networking opportunity to establish a relationship with HDR students in their faculties.

Library evaluation of these sessions has been undertaken by an online survey sent by e-mail. The feedback was to gauge how participants felt about the sessions as well as self assessment of the development of their research skills. The results of the survey were very positive. They reported an increase in skills and knowledge across all areas of the training. Some students chose to repeat some sessions to fully appreciate the content. The programme will be refined, based on participant and presenter feedback, and re-presented.

Institute of Koorie Education

The Institute of Koorie Education is a unique and exemplary model of community-based learning designed to enable Aboriginal and Torres Strait Islander students to study without being removed from their communities for substantial periods of time. This natural synergy with Deakin University Library's culture of inclusivity and flexible delivery has been strengthened by partnerships between liaison librarians and lecturers to achieve personalised student centred support.

The Australian Government acknowledges that these students are 'significantly under-represented in our universities and face distinct challenges' (Australia, 2009). However, the institute's approach promotes access and equity for more than 500 Indigenous students from all areas of Australia enrolled across a broad range of units.

Students attend on-campus intensive study blocks, during which students stay on site at the Kitjarra residences located at the Geelong campus at Waurn Ponds, and off-campus service delivery is complemented by local tutors at regional study centres. The central philosophy of the Institute is underpinned by customised teaching styles, flexible time-tabling arrangements and high quality support offered by close links with students during their educational journey. To be an effective partner the library has also embraced this support style.

There is no substitute, or short cut, to open communication and personal contact to get the best results for these students.

Initially library support took the form of instruction and reassurance in relation to requesting subject based resources via the library catalogue or by phone when the students were at home, often in remote parts of the country. However, institute enrolments have since increased. The range of degrees offered has expanded across all four faculties including Arts and Education, Business and Law, Health and Science, and there has been a higher emphasis placed on research, all of which has prompted the development of closer relationships with individual liaison librarians. Meeting new, continuing and casual academic staff at the institute requires an ongoing commitment to communication but as a result library staff have a better understanding of the needs and experience of this client group.

There are multiple course entry and exit points, deferment and full and part time study options to allow this largely mature age cohort to structure study around work and lifestyle. The library works within the Institute preference for small, interactive learning groups, culturally inclusive curriculum and a non competitive and supportive learning environment. Liaison librarians now actively collaborate with institute staff to develop orientation by faculty for students when they are on campus for intensive teaching blocks. Research skills instruction related to forthcoming assignments are given in the library to small groups. This is an ideal teaching environment as feedback is immediate and content can be flexible and relevant. Liaison librarians also make themselves available to see students individually, either in the library, at the institute, or over at the Kitjarra residences.

Good communication with the institute, and the ability to be flexible within the demands of their timetable, are necessary to ensure that the specific needs of students are met in the short and busy time that they are on campus.

Ms Brenda Brodie, lecturer in Arts and Education, had this to say:

- ... Koorie students are being encouraged to use the library and to use it well, which then flows through into their research activities.

- The Waurn Ponds Library Staff are approachable and helpful and have encouraged staff at the Institute to use them in arranging workshops for a range of activities and have responded quickly and positively to requests for library orientation tours for small and large groups that are tailored to specific disciplines, for specific workshops/ presentations in speciality areas.

The aim is also to reinforce that personal contact and online library help is never far away when students return to their communities, sometimes in remote areas of Australia, so e-mail support is also well used.

> You have no idea how much your quick response, support and expertise meant ... I would like to say THANK YOU.
>
> I appreciate your genuine care. You are definitely on the side of the angels. (Bachelor of Laws student)

At a recent Institute of Koorie Education Graduation we heard students' personal testimonials, including their plans to use new-found expertise and leadership within their communities. Celebrating their achievements with other academic support team members was further affirmation of the impact successful partnerships can have on student engagement.

Conclusion

Each of the partnerships outlined above has developed as a response to client needs. However, working collaboratively has strengthened each relationship and allowed the breakdown of traditional sectional silos for mutually beneficial outcomes. Close communication between the library and its partners within the university has built respect for the different but complementary skills of academics and liaison librarians. The result has enabled enhanced teaching and learning. It appears that this communication is best, at least initially, face to face to encourage the understanding and trust of personal relationships to develop, which can then be the catalyst for exciting opportunities for student engagement. There can be no better interpretation of the liaison link.

Note

1. An equity group is a phrase used in Australia to cover groups of people who have traditionally not had a high participation

rate in higher education. These groups include people from non-English speaking backgrounds, with disabilities, from rural or isolated areas, from socio-economically disadvantaged backgrounds, or of Aboriginal or Torres Strait Islander descent.

References

Australia, EaWR Department of Education (2009) *Transforming Australia's Higher Education System*, Australia, Australian Government.

Deakin University (2010) *Deakin University Strategic Plan: Delivering effective partnerships 2010*, Melbourne.

Deakin University Library (2009) Liaison Services review Working Group 2009 *Final report: Liaison Services Review 2008–2009*, Deakin University.

Doskatsch, I. (2003) 'Perceptions and perplexities of the faculty-librarian partnership: an Australian perspective', *Reference Service Review*, vol. 31, no. 2, pp. 111–21, via Emerald.

Lingham, B. (2010) *Report on Library research training for Higher Degree by Research Students February – May 2010*, Deakin University.

Rodwell, J. and Fairbairn, L. (2008) 'Dangerous liaisons? Defining the faculty liaison librarian service model, its effectiveness and sustainability', *Library Management*, vol. 29, no. 1/2, pp. 116–124, via Emerald, available at *www.emeraldinsight.com/journals.htm?articleid=1641759&show=abstract*.

17

Where are we now?

Abstract: This chapter reviews the present situation of libraries and their role with clients at both ends of the wealth spectrum in a climate of cuts in public spending. It considers how librarians are adjusting to their role, transformed by ICT, and reminds them that their traditional role has not disappeared – merely mutated.

Key words: changes in library use, ICT, traditional librarian values, cuts in library expenditure.

But our job as information scientists is not to criticize people for being as they are but to design services for them. I have never been happy about trying to redesign human beings to fit information services. (Line, 1999)

Across the globe, the work of librarians embraces a world of strange extremes, from servicing the needs of the richest nations on earth to assisting the very poorest in the world to access knowledge and culture. This book has considered a variety of causes, social, economic and political, which set up barriers to communication between librarians and their client groups and lead to possible exclusion from the world of information.

For the many, usually younger, information seekers in the affluent parts of the world, Marshall McLuhan so prophetically stated: 'The medium is the message' (McLuhan, 1964); i.e. a medium affects the society where it plays a role, not only by the content it delivers, but also by the characteristics of the medium itself.

Librarians adapting to new technologies

The very *positive* aspects of online availability of resources and the possibility of interactions outside of normal time and space constraints offer many advantages which should not be underestimated; librarians across the globe are recognising these possibilities and are embracing them in a thoughtful, considered way. They acknowledge that the online reference interview should still bear some resemblance to the face-to-face reference interview. In an online interaction, even in real time, the lack of a physical presence of one's interlocutor can never be fully compensated, although other possibilities exist for representing the important elements of a good reference interview. We can attempt to compensate for the lack of the facial gestures and body language present in a face-to-face interview, e.g. a smile or leaning forward to show interest and friendliness. Using the enquirer's name, if known, is a sign of friendliness: Ronan (2003) gives sound advice by reminding us to 'greet a person named Steve with a "Hello Steve. How may I help you?" ... One very common error I've noticed new staff making is immediately starting to search for an answer to the initial question without greeting the user who has just logged on'. This is a clever rapport-building shift from the smile, the universally accepted act for building trust and cooperation to the use of the client's own name, again universally acknowledged as strengthening rapport. As Carnegie (1937) reminded us: 'Remember that a person's name is to that person the sweetest and most important sound in any language.'

Ronan (2003) also reminds us: 'One of the biggest challenges in providing reference services in real-time is learning to communicate effectively with remote users and to translate the interpersonal skills used at the physical reference desk into the virtual environment'. We need to remember that people are only human. Information and communication technology is wonderful but does not fully replace human contact. Sproull and Kiesler (1985) considered Computer Mediated Communication to be an impoverished communication experience, with the reduction of available social cues resulting in a greater sense or feeling of anonymity. This in turn is said to have a deindividuating effect on the individuals involved, producing behaviour that is more self-centred and less socially regulated than usual. This reduced-information model of Internet communication assumes further that the reduction of social cues, compared to richer face-to-face situations, must necessarily have negative effects on social interaction (i.e. a weaker, relatively impoverished social interaction). Ford (2004) found that in-person interactions were overall 'richer' than virtual interactions, with e-mail interactions quite low in interactivity, and chat more like face-to face interactions. Nilsen (2006) reports that 'virtual reference transaction accounts (both e-mail and chat) show that virtual reference results in lower satisfaction than in-person reference.' These results may be due to the librarians observed being ill at ease with the technology and forgetting the basic principles of conducting a reference interview: 80 per cent of those observed failed to do so, compared with 49 per cent of face-to-face transactions observed. It is interesting to note that the face-to-face interaction per se is far from perfection; however, the technology seems to have provided yet another barrier!

Librarian failure to communicate well in the virtual environment has also been observed by Walter and Mediavilla (2005), who report that librarians were clearly uncomfortable in the chat discourse environment and sought to distance themselves from their teenage clients who 'attempted to create meaning by recreating the chat discourse environment in which they were most at home'.

Digital reference guidelines

The IFLA Digital Reference Guidelines (2008), which make reference to the RUSA Reference Guidelines (2004), advise librarians, inter alia, to 'Use spelling, grammar and capitalization appropriately – "chat speak" is generally more conversational than formally written prose' and to 'Type like you talk, in a conversational manner'.

As with any librarian-client encounter there can be a variation in quality of interactions, both in terms of information provided and the manner of service delivery. Radford (2006) made a comparison, based on the analysis of transcripts, of the interpersonal communication on chat reference services between potentially award-winning transcripts[1] and transcripts selected at random.

Negative aspects of online interaction

A more general manifestation of this failure of the virtual to satisfy the basic human need for contact is the loneliness reported by the Facebook generation: they may be more 'connected' than ever, but loneliness is a problem even among young people. Loneliness has been associated with increased Internet use (Morahan-Martin and Schumacher, 2003).

A recent survey by the Samaritans found that young people worried more about loneliness than even the elderly: 21 per cent of those aged between 18 and 24 said that it was one of their main worries, compared with 8 per cent of over-55s ... The trend has been highlighted by a new website that offers visitors the chance to purchase friends on social networking sites such as Facebook and Twitter. (Ahmed and Hamilton, 2009)

Notwithstanding these problems which, for some, may be aggravated by online encounters, for many, online communication is merely an *alternative* one, at times preferable in terms of convenience. It has been said that some librarians have been reluctant to embrace fully the new modes of communicating with clients, in a kind of inverted snobbery. It is true that the young are often more impressed by the technological means of a communication than by the quality of the content, e.g. accepting as accurate anything received via the Internet – a bizarre echo of how years ago people used to claim veracity for a statement by saying, 'It's true. I read it in a book.'

Librarians need to be sceptical of the inflated reports of the expertise of the Google generation: a report commissioned by JISC and the British Library researchers found that although young people demonstrate an ease and familiarity with computers, they rely on the most basic search tools and do not possess the critical and analytical skills to assess the information that they find on the web. The report also gives the lie to the myth that reading books is in decline: in the UK people read more in 2007 than they did in 1975 (Williams and Rowlands, 2007).

However, clinging only to the traditional is not an option for a good librarian: 'our job as information scientists is not to criticize people for being as they are but to design services for them' (Line, 1999).

There is evidence of librarians wholeheartedly espousing the new channels of communication: 'Emergent Technologies in Education' is an exciting professional development programme in emerging technologies for librarians at the University of Western Australia, set up in 2008 to address a lack of pedagogically grounded training in this area.

> A qualitative analysis of participants' online contributions and course projects, complemented by quantitative survey data, reveals that most librarians acquired new understandings of both pedagogy and technology; many were able to apply newly gained skills in the workplace; and some went on to create pedagogically grounded, technologically enabled resources of ongoing value to the library. (Pegrum and Kiel, 2011)

Disadvantage is still present

In stark contrast to this wealth of high tech provision for the affluent, are the realities of the cutbacks in public expenditure which will serve to exacerbate the disadvantage of those already disadvantaged. In the UK, at the time of writing, the threat of closure menaces many public libraries. In largely rural Gloucestershire this means over half, including the mobile ones which service remote communities. The author Joanna Trollope (2011) appeals:

> I hope they both have the wit and grace to listen and to change their minds, before Gloucestershire becomes a byword for depriving the very people who need the service most. We know there has to be a new library

strategy for these difficult times. We know some financial pruning has to take place. But why take your biggest axe to the one tree that (cheaply) gives more oxygen to the inner lives and aspirations of a whole county, especially its disadvantaged, than any other?

Given that for some the only chance of their accessing the Internet is at the public library, the implications are serious. As recently as December 2010, it was reported that there are '3 million UK children still without computers or broadband ISP internet access' in the UK (ISP Review, 2010) in their own homes – arguably a minority in a country with a total population of 61 million (of which a fifth are children), but an important minority at a potentially crippling disadvantage, if not catered for in libraries. Among developed countries, the UK is unlikely to be the only one in which some children are deprived of access to the latest technology.

It is gratifying to note that, at the time of writing, in some parts of the UK, people are demonstrating their appreciation of libraries and are fighting against planned library closures. Interestingly, in defence of books they are making use of the latest technology:

> The library at Stony Stratford, on the outskirts of Milton Keynes, looks like the aftermath of a crime, its shell-shocked staff presiding over an expanse of emptied shelves. Only a few days ago they held 16,000 volumes. Now, after a campaign on Facebook ... there are none. Every library user was urged to pick their full entitlement of 15 books, take them away and keep them for a week ... One man stopped me in the street and said, 'The library is the one place where you find five-year-olds and 90-year-olds together, and it's where young people learn to be proper citizens'. (Kennedy, 2011)

At the very extreme of the spectrum are those people so disconnected that they do not have a roof of their own, let alone a fast Internet connection, but are still being offered access to information and culture through books. The vision of the Footpath library, started in Australia in 2003 is 'to empower homeless and disadvantaged people through books. The Benjamin Andrew Footpath Library achieves this vision by delivering a regular supply of books to homeless and disadvantaged people living in hostels and on the streets, and through community organizations. (Benjamin Andrew Footpath Library, 2011)

Our guiding principles

Librarians need to remain flexible and versatile. On the one hand we must move with the times and be a fully functioning part of those times, by being conversant with and able to interact in the latest communication technology. On the other hand we must not forget our guiding principles and should seek to communicate with, and indeed sometimes on behalf of, the less advantaged and articulate of our potential clientele. 'One of the distinguishing features of professions is that their knowledge and skills are at the service of society at large, and do not simply serve the interests of the immediate customer' and this may even involve being a whistle blower: 'Members who are employed have duties that go beyond the immediate terms of their employment contract. On occasion these may conflict with the immediate demands of their employer but be in the broader interest of the public and possibly the employer themselves' (CILIP, 2009).

Note

1. 44 transcripts nominated for the LSSI Samuel Swett Green Award for Exemplary Virtual Reference.

References

Ahmed, M. and Hamilton, F. (2009) 'Facebook is adding to problem of loneliness, say Samaritans', *Times*, 31 December 2009.

Benjamin Andrew Footpath Library website, *www.footpathlibrary.org/* (accessed 11/01/11).

Carnegie, D. (1937) *How to win friends and influence people*, New York: Simon and Schuster.

CILIP (2009) 'Code of Professional Practice for Library and Information Professionals', available at: *www.cilip.org.uk/get-involved/policy/ethics/pages/code.aspx* (accessed 11/01/11).

Ford (2004) 'Doctoral dissertation fellowship winner explores the difference between face-to-face and computer-mediated reference interactions', *College and Research Libraries News*, 65, 11, p. 645.

IFLA (2008) 'IFLA Digital Reference Guidelines', available at *http://archive.ifla.org/VII/s36/pubs/drg03.htm* (accessed 12/01/11).

ISP Review (2010) *www.ispreview.co.uk/story/2010/12/28/3-million-uk-children-still-without-computers-or-broadband-isp-internet-access.html* (accessed 15/01/10).

Kennedy, M. (2011) 'Library clears its shelves in protest at closure threat', *Guardian*, 15 January 2011, available at *www.guardian.co.uk/books/2011/jan/14/stony-stratford-library-shelves-protest* (accessed 22/01/11).

Line, M.B. (1999) 'Social Science information – the poor relation', *INSPEL*, 33 (3), pp. 131–6.

McLuhan, M. (1964) *Understanding Media: The Extensions of Man*, New York: McGraw-Hill.

Morahan-Martin, J. and Phyllis Schumacher, P. (2003) 'Loneliness and social uses of the internet', *Computers in Human Behavior*, 19 (6), pp. 659–71.

Nilsen, K. (2006) 'Comparing users' perspectives of in-person and virtual reference', *New Library World* 107,1222/1223, pp. 91–4, available at *www.emeraldinsight.com/0307-4803.htm* (accessed 2/01/11).

Pegrum, M. and Kiel, R. (2011) '"Changing the way we talk": Developing librarians' competence in emerging technologies through a structured program', College & Research Libraries, in press. Preprint *http://crl.acrl.org/content/early/2010/12/23/crl-190.full.pdf+html* (accessed 15/01/11).

Radford, M.L. (2006) 'Encouraging virtual users: a qualitative investigation of interpersonal communication in chat reference', *Journal of the American Society for Information Science and Technology*, 57, 8, pp. 1046–59.

Ronan, J. (2003) 'The reference interview online', *Reference and User Services Quarterly*, 43, 1, pp. 43–7.

RUSA (2004) 'Guidelines for Behavioral Performance of Reference and Information Service Providers', available at *www.ala.org/Template.cfm?Section=Home&template=/ContentManagement/ContentDisplay.cfm&Content ID=26937* (accessed 12/01/11).

Sproull, L. and Kiesler, S. (1985) 'Reducing social context cues: electronic mail in organizational communication', *Manag. Sci.*, 11, 1, pp. 492–512.

Trollope, J. (2011) 'The library cuts in Gloucestershire go beyond necessity or common sense. The county council is taking the axe to an inexpensive service that helps its most deprived people', *Guardian*, 8 January 2011, available from *www.guardian.co.uk/books/2011/jan/07/library-cuts-gloucestershire-joanna-trollope* (accessed 11/01/11).

Walter, V.A. and Mediavillia, C. (2005) 'Teens are from Neptune, librarians are from Pluto: an analysis of online reference transactions', *Library Trends*, 54, 2, pp. 209–27.

Williams, P. and Rowlands, I. (2007) Information behaviour of the researcher of the future. A British Library/JISC study. The literature on young people and their information behaviour. Work package II.

Index